I0170105

Without My Father

A year of mourning and reflection

Daniel Rose

Clink
Street

London | New York

This book is dedicated to the beloved memory of my father,
Mark Maurice Rose, Mordechai Moshe Ben Arieh.
May his memory forever be a blessing.

For my Mother, Ruth, with eternal gratitude
for her love, support and wisdom.

For my children, Natan and Yaniv,
who bring me so much pride.

Contents

If by attending shul and reciting the kaddish prayer, was even in the slightest way helping my father's journey, then it was not in my nature to even question what I was doing.

Prologue

Wednesday, 26th August 2015

The plane touched down on the tarmac at Ben Gurion Airport. As some of the passengers started to clap (a usual occurrence when landing in Israel), I glanced at my parents who were both smiling. I had gotten divorced in the January of that year and was still adjusting to not being with my two sons every day. My sons had gone away that week with their mother, and when my parents invited me to join them in Israel for a week's holiday, I jumped at the chance.

Dad had been lacking in any sort of energy lately, and I was relieved when he chose to hitch a ride in the buggy to passport control with Mum. We arrived in Netanya at approximately 7 pm. There was some sort of a festival going on, and it took the taxi driver a while to navigate through the crowd to get to the front of the hotel.

Once we were in our rooms, I was hoping we would venture out for dinner, but Dad was clearly exhausted. I went downstairs to get falafel in pitta for everyone, which we ate in my parents' room. I assumed that Dad just needed a good night's sleep and would feel better in the morning.

My parents spent most of their time at the hotel pool, napped in the afternoons and went out to local places for dinner. I spent most of my days at the beach and catching up with friends.

Friday, 28th August sticks in my mind for a variety of reasons. Dad would always go to shul (synagogue) on Friday night when in Israel, but he felt too tired to go this time. I met my parents in their room, and we went downstairs to the hotel restaurant for dinner. Dad turned to me and asked me to make kiddush (the blessing over the wine, ushering in the Sabbath). I was shocked. Dad had never asked me to make kiddush on his behalf. He was very much of the opinion that as 'head of the family' it was his right and I had never really given it much thought. I asked him why and he said that he was finding it difficult to remember the words. Dad had made kiddush for us as a family and for Mum on every Shabbat and Chag (Jewish holiday) for our entire lives and I was very concerned at this admission but at the time I put it down to tiredness and old age. I made kiddush and we enjoyed a nice meal together.

Towards the end of my stay I had encouraged Mum and Dad to come to the beach with me for a swim. It did take some persuasion, but there was a lift that we could get down the cliff, avoiding the stairs, so they finally agreed. I helped Mum into the sea and a wave immediately knocked her over. I rushed to help her up and to my delight she was laughing and I guided her to some calmer water (at the request of the lifeguard who was shouting at me).

Dad had also gone for a swim. Just before we left the beach, he walked up to the sea, hands behind his back and gazed thoughtfully out at the horizon for about five minutes. I took a picture of him. To this day I wish I had asked him what he was thinking about.

Four months later my father passed away.

Chapter 1
Denial and Acceptance

1

It must have been in October of 2015 that the vomiting started. Dad had been feeling increasingly tired and weak. I wasn't too concerned and again put it down to old age, but the vomiting continued with no signs of letting up. I was also worried that my mother, who not in the best of health, was doing her best to look after Dad and was having to clear up the vomit at all hours of the day and night. The vomiting did not let up and Mum eventually called an ambulance. The paramedics assessed my father and took him to A&E at Barnet Hospital. As soon as I heard, I drove down there and my sister Abigail did the same. The doctor, after the usual waiting for many hours did a few tests on my father and dismissed him with a case of having a stomach virus. We were all relieved that there was nothing more sinister and I took my parents home.

The vomiting did not stop and my parents decided to see a private doctor to get some more tests done. I can recall Mum on the phone to the doctor and being told that he had an appointment available that Friday evening. Mum responded that it was the Jewish Sabbath and they would be unable to attend and she made an appointment for the following week. As soon as Mum got off the phone I told her to phone straight back and make the appointment for Friday night and that I would drive them there and back. Dad agreed much to my amazement – for him to get in a car on Shabbat was unthinkable and made us realise how worried he must have been to have ever agreed to this.

Once again my sister Abigail joined us and a variety of tests were done on Dad. The doctor called him the following week on the 25th November. He was very concerned about my father's blood levels which he said were off the scale and that he had written a letter, and Dad needed to get himself admitted to A&E at Barnet hospital again for further tests and a possible blood transfusion.

Dad had never been in hospital overnight before except for that same year in May when he had had a pacemaker fitted. We waited as usual for a long time in triage until he was eventually seen by a doctor and was finally allocated a room in a ward upstairs. We accompanied him there and made sure he was settled. He was so tired and lay in bed with his eyes closed with Mum holding his hand. He was put on an IV drip the following day and also given a blood transfusion. The next few days consisted of picking up my mother and heading to the hospital and doing our best to keep Dad's spirits up. I still did not think at this point that there was anything majorly wrong and can even remember with Mum, discussing with the doctor our concerns over Dad's driving which had become increasingly worse over the years.

Then the bombshell: 'We have discovered a shadow on your pancreas. But at this point we are more concerned about stabilising your blood levels.' Even at this time I was still in denial. I didn't have a clue what the pancreas was or what purpose it served. I shared the doctor's concern that the first priority was sorting out the blood levels, and the mass detected on the pancreas would be sorted at a later date.

2

Dad's strength continued to lessen. He had been unable to keep a meal down for a long time. The doctors were trying to bulk him up with a liquid diet but he was finding it hard to even consume one carton. His legs had virtually no strength in them and the nurses were helping him to try to walk again, steadying him as he held on to a walker. The days continued to pass and I was doing my best to juggle my commitments to my children and spend as much time at hospital with Dad as I could.

My parents had brought us up in an orthodox household but I continued to visit him – even on Shabbat. I couldn't stand the thought of him spending all day alone. I was living in Collier Row at the time. The first time I appeared on Shabbat I was worried he would tell me off but he was just happy to see me and did not mention the day.

I tried to carry on during this time as best I could. I took the children to the cinema one night and even went to a fancy dress party for a friend's 40th and I recall taking my eldest son Natan to Imax to see the new James Bond movie, which I had booked months earlier followed by a meal at Reubens in Baker Street.

On the 9th December 2015, Dad was discharged from hospital. The doctors had been talking about him going home for a while and we had discussed palliative care. On one occasion I had left the hospital to meet someone at my parents' house to install a few items to make things easier for Dad on his return home. All I can really remember was a device to go over the toilet seat with a handrail to enable Dad to ease himself up more easily. The man who delivered the items was in the house for less than half an hour and I then drove back to Barnet Hospital.

I was pleased that Dad was going home. I knew he would be more comfortable and steady in familiar surroundings but I was worried about Mum and how she was going to cope with looking after him. So far, Mum had been fantastic in staying with Dad every day in hospital and coping with the late evenings, but I knew that sooner or later it would all catch up with her. Dad was discharged that evening. It was a cold, rainy Wednesday night and we packed up Dad's belongings. He was helped into a wheelchair and I wheeled him down to the hospital reception and left him with Mum so that I could bring the car nearer to the entrance. Dad was in his dressing gown and slippers. He hadn't had the energy to get dressed. I couldn't help thinking that it might have been better for him to stay one more night rather than discharging him so late in the evening, but he was so relieved to be going home that I couldn't help but be happy for him. I wheeled him over to the car and had to practically lift him up and lower him into the car seat. I was horrified at how light he felt and was concerned at how he was going to manage at home if he couldn't lift himself out of the wheelchair. We arrived back at my parent's house in Southgate. I double parked outside and once again I had to almost lift Dad out of the car and then helped him into the house and into a chair at the dining table. I went back outside to find a place to park and entered the house again. It was the fourth night of Chanukah (an eight day festival which celebrates the reclaiming of the Holy Temple in Jerusalem by a small band of Jews, led by Judah Macabee, which was then rededicated to the service of G-d) and the first thing we did was light the Chanukiah and sing Hanerot Halalu and Ma'oz Tzur. It was so nice to see Dad back home and heart-warming to see that the first thing he wanted to do was celebrate Chanukah back in his own home. I hung around for a bit but knew that Dad just wanted to go to bed so I gave him a hug and told him how pleased I was that he was back home again. I gave Mum a kiss and left.

That was the last night Dad would sleep at home.

3

I got home that night feeling exhausted as usual and went to bed shortly after. The next morning I called to see how he was doing. The news from Mum wasn't good. Dad was vomiting uncontrollably again. Mum called an ambulance and I headed straight over. When I got there, I found Dad sitting in a chair in the bedroom. He was trying to make light of the situation and even placed a cardboard carton from the hospital over his head wondering if it would suit him as a hat. We really didn't want Dad to go back to hospital but knew he could not carry on like this.

The ambulance took almost five hours to arrive. The paramedics (especially the female one) were very caring. They were horrified that he had been discharged in that state, which left me feeling upset. They helped Dad out to the ambulance. Mum got in with him and I locked up the house and headed towards Barnet Hospital again, phoning my sisters and aunt en route to update them.

We arrived to complete chaos. There were so many people waiting to be admitted via ambulance that we had no choice but to wait with Dad in a very draughty corridor between the ambulance entrance and A&E. Dad looked terrible. He wasn't talking much and I was trying to chat to him to keep his spirits up. The paramedic was fantastic and kept chatting with Dad and kept her hand reassuringly on his shoulder. My sister had arrived by now and I was comforted to see her. She was trying to cheer Mum up and engage us in conversation. Dad was finally admitted into the assessment area and a doctor once again came to see him. This doctor seemed to have actually read the notes and said he needed to be back on the ward. Dad was feeling really cold, despite the heat inside the hospital and I took my coat off and placed it over his chest. It must have been almost midnight at this point and I suggested that Abigail take our mother home and get some sleep and I would stay with Dad. It was almost 2 am by the time a bed was found and I accompanied him up to the ward and unpacked his things. Dad got into bed and I kissed him goodnight before heading home.

The next few days were much the same with more blood transfusions and drips. Dad was really grateful to family and friends who dropped by to see him. He was transferred to another ward. I took my children as often as I could to visit but I didn't really want them to see Dad in such a weak condition. The days were very long and I sometimes did Dad's crossword puzzles – asking for his help whenever I was stumped. My ex-wife was really kind during this time and looked after the kids as often as she could so that I could be at the hospital. My sister did something so kind and thoughtful. She knew how important it was for Dad to light the Chanukah candles. Obviously the hospital would not allow flames on the ward so Abigail bought some electric tea lights which we could light together with him and celebrate Chanukah. I remember one night with our children singing Ma'oz Tzur next to his bed and the look of happiness on Dad's face with his grandchildren around him. It was also nice to see a Chanukiah in the reception at the hospital celebrating each day of Chanukah.

The doctors said that there was not much they could do with my father at Barnet Hospital and they were going to transfer him to a different hospital where they could provide more specialist care to him and also look into the possibility of fitting a stent so that they could bypass the blockage in the pancreas and hopefully start building some muscle mass in him again.

4

Dad was transferred during the night of 19th December and was operated on the following morning to fit the stent. By the time I arrived with Mum he was already in surgery. I had been told that the operation would take approximately an hour. We waited in the family area for over two hours and received no news. I started to panic and pace the room. Finally they wheeled Dad out on a bed. He was still unconscious from the anaesthetic and Mum and I walked with him back to the ward, meeting my sister along the way. His cubicle was next to the entrance of the ward. We sat around his bed waiting for him to wake up.

Eventually his eyes opened and he turned to look at Abigail. She grinned at him in her cheeky way and Dad was comforted to see her smile. By this time, my other sister, Emma, and most of the immediate family had turned up, including my brothers-in-law, Aviv and David.

Dad needed to go to the bathroom. He was still quite disorientated and I went to get a nurse. Two of them came and closed the curtain around his bed to give him some privacy and we all (except for Mum) waited by the ward entrance. Suddenly there was a loud bang. We turned to look and Dad had fallen over just outside the curtain. I rushed over to him and put my arms around him from behind to support him and was about to pick him up and let him sit on the bed. The nurses told me not to and that they would need to find a commode or a wheelchair. They also told me not to lift him as I may hurt myself. I responded with 'He's not your father.' They wandered off with no sense of urgency or care leaving me on the floor with Dad. I held him tight and told him to lean back against me. To this day, I feel so much anger that they asked the family to leave the ward so they could look after him. There were two of them and they obviously let Dad, coming around from an anaesthetic, get out of bed by himself and fall to the floor. I was shocked at their lack of care and urgency. They eventually returned and I lifted Dad and placed him in the wheelchair. Later that evening, Dad was brought a meal – some soup and a bread roll. My sister checked with the doctor if he was allowed to eat the bread. The doctor said that he could and Dad actually ate with some enthusiasm. Later on the vomiting started again. When we spoke with another doctor on the following day, she said that Dad should never have been given the bread roll to eat. Again, we were furious at the wrong advice being given. I believe this is the last time that Dad tried to eat anything of substance.

5

The days were unrelenting. It was taking far longer to get to the new hospital from Collier Row (or from Southgate on the days when I collected Mum first). I was grateful on the days that my sisters were able to collect Mum in the mornings and we would always make sure between us that she was able to get home in the evenings. During this time Mum's older sister Madeleine was a fantastic support to us. She practically put her life on hold and visited almost every day and was a constant source of reassurance to all of us. Something I will always remember. Nobody expected her to make the trip every day on public transport but she did – even when we suggested that it was too much for her.

I had emailed Dad's Rabbi, Daniel Epstein from Cockfosters and North Southgate Shul, to let him know that Dad was in hospital. He was grateful for the information and I was a little surprised that none of Dad's friends had passed this information to him. Rabbi Epstein visited Dad on that very day and continued to visit him and stay in touch with me even after Dad was transferred. I was deeply appreciative of the time he must have been taking out of a very busy schedule.

By this time a doctor had confirmed to us that Dad had a nasty mass on his pancreas and that they were looking into possible treatments. I had googled the symptoms and knew that there was no treatment that could possibly cure this condition – especially at my father's age and in his weakened state. I was hoping at this point that perhaps chemo could help him. I read up on the statistics on survival rates and knew that Dad had virtually no chance of surviving this. All of the symptoms that he had had over the last month were consistent with this disease and I found it difficult to comprehend how nobody had recognised the symptoms and been able to diagnose this any earlier. The pancreas is difficult to access on an x-ray – hidden behind other organs which is another reason why diagnosis is usually too late for any effective treatment to be given. We were also told that Dad had caught pneumonia – a side effect of pancreatic cancer. I couldn't help but think that he may have caught this with the long wait in the draughty corridor for all those hours whilst being admitted back to Barnet hospital for the second time. But who knew? They put him on a strong antibiotic drip to try and help with this.

6

It was on the 23rd December that Dad took a turn for the worse. He had texted me every morning at exactly 8.30 am to let me know he was ok and I had messaged back and then called Mum to let her know he had messaged and would be leaving shortly to pick her up. On this day no text arrived. I called the hospital ward and asked whoever answered the phone to check on my father to see if he was ok. I explained that he messaged me every morning but that no message has arrived. She told me that they were busy and to call back in half an hour. I was shocked at this attitude. Dad's ward was right opposite the nurse's station. It would have taken them thirty seconds to check on him. I hung up the phone, got in the car and headed straight to Mum. I called her on the way, explaining what had happened and asked her to be ready as soon as I arrived. She got in the car and we drove to the hospital.

When we arrived on the ward, we knew something was majorly wrong. Dad looked at us with no recognition and was not speaking. His eyes were blank. We tried to talk to him but to no avail. I went outside to try and locate a doctor but no one was around. I finally grabbed a doctor who came onto the ward. I explained the situation but he told me that he was by himself that day, a lot of doctors were absent and he had no idea about my father's case – nor was it likely that he would even be able to read his notes until at least 4 pm. I was horrified and went outside the ward trying to collect myself and calm down. Two senior nurses must have seen the expression on my face and asked me what was wrong. I told them how disgusted I was that nobody had checked on my father that morning when I had phoned and how the only doctor who visited the ward had no idea about my father's case. They both took my arm and led me into a private room. They said the doctor had no right to tell me that and asked me who I had spoken on the phone with that morning. I replied that I didn't know – I had been too worried to ask for the name and wanted to know if my father could be examined any earlier. I had a nasty suspicion that he may have suffered a stroke. The nurses couldn't calm me down and I went back to the ward and started a war of words on Twitter.

It's astonishing how Twitter can get such a quick response. The digital communications manager responded to me via email and said she had passed my email onto the deputy director of nursing for my father's ward who was currently speaking to the matron. Eventually we got seen. I asked some rather blunt questions including how long Dad had left. We were told he may have six months. I had expected this but it was still a shock to hear and I remember grabbing onto my mother's hand.

7

I knew at this stage that my father may not have long to go but to actually hear it confirmed by a doctor was like being hit by a bus. My sister Abigail turned up shortly after and we broke the news to her. I needed to be alone for a while and made my way outside the ward and sat down on a bench. Abigail sat down next to me and cried and hugged me. I hadn't even noticed her exit the ward but I was very glad of her company. Just then my other sister Emma turned up and we broke the news to her.

By this time Dad was unable to pass water and had to have a catheter fitted but he didn't seem to be able to comprehend this and kept trying to get out of bed. It was becoming a huge emotional struggle to get him to stay in bed and we all did our best to reassure him that he didn't have to move. We all needed each other for moral support.

Dad was sometimes able to chat and communicate but at other times he would drift in and out of sleep. He would stare into space and suddenly start talking. One time he told me that if he was not well enough by Purim (over three months away) that I was to use his megillah scroll – one of his most prized possessions. Purim is a Jewish holiday that commemorates the saving of the Jewish people in ancient Persia from Haman, who was planning to kill all the Jews. We read the megillah (the story of Esther) twice. My father had a handwritten scroll that he loved to use. I told him that of course he would be well enough and I would go with him to shul and we could read it together. I knew this wouldn't happen. Our parents had booked for all of us to accompany them to Israel for Pesach (The Passover holiday which celebrates the Jewish people being released from slavery in Egypt). It was something we had all been looking forward to. Dad told me that if he wasn't well enough that he wanted us to all go. I discussed this with my mother and sister. We agreed that if Dad was still around that there was no way we could leave him alone during this time. With their permission I phoned the travel agent and cancelled the holiday. I found it very hard to find the words to explain why. We also needed to find the right time to let Dad know what the doctor had said about his diagnosis. We never did get the opportunity to tell him, for which I am now glad.

The days were really starting to take their toll on us. Mum was getting increasingly tired. My sisters were trying to juggle their children and visit Dad as often as possible. I was having a long drive in the mornings and evenings and trying to be strong for both my parents and have enough energy to look after my children on the nights they stayed with me.

On Christmas day, my one thought was that parking at the hospital may be easier. It wasn't.

27th December. Dad had always loved his chicken soup. Although he could not eat any solids by this point and was on a feeding tube, I hoped that the smell of the soup may persuade him to have some. I made the soup at home in the usual way but when it was ready I strained it and portioned it into some small plastic tubs. The next day I took them into the hospital. Dad was sitting up in bed and I asked him if he would like some chicken soup and he nodded. I asked a nurse to heat it up and she brought it back. He tried to grip the spoon but I could see he didn't have the strength to bring the spoon to his mouth so I asked him if he would like me to do it. Dad nodded again and I managed to feed about four spoons of soup to him before he lost interest. I was disappointed in how little he managed but at least he had had some.

8

A few days later a doctor asked to speak to Mum and me. We went into a room and he gave Mum a form and asked her that when the time came, they would like her written consent not to resuscitate. We looked at each other. I could feel my heart racing and I breathed deeply trying to control my emotions. My first reaction was not to sign. Dad was getting weaker, he was sleeping a lot more and not eating and was a shadow of his former self. I believed that asking to resuscitate would be cruel and only prolong his suffering. I whispered to my mother that she should sign it and she did. At this point I believed he only had perhaps two weeks left and was not holding out hope for six months as the doctor had suggested.

From this point my health started to go downhill. I was constantly tired and had started suffering with panic attacks. I went to the doctor and asked for help and I was prescribed Valium and put on antidepressants. The dosage of the antidepressants was increased shortly after.

5th January 2016. My mother carried a book of psalms on her and sometimes read from it and said it had helped her through difficult times. She suggested that I get one too. We were going to stop off in Finchley Road at a Jewish bookshop on the way to the hospital and were driving down Ballards Lane when Mum mentioned that perhaps it was time to ask the Rabbi to recite the Viduy, 'The confession', for my father. This prayer is traditionally recited on one's death bed, preparing the soul on leaving this world to the next and asking forgiveness for any transgressions. I felt the panic rising. Suppose Dad got scared that he was going to die. Perhaps we were reciting the prayer too early. I couldn't admit out loud that Dad didn't have long left. I remained silent but the panic was rising.

We stopped off at the bookshop and purchased my book. I was trying my best to remain calm and was breathing deeply but felt like I was about to pass out. We walked out to the car and I opened the door for my mother and walked around the back of the car and an uncontrollable wave of emotions took over me. I got in the car and burst into tears. I couldn't breathe and was gasping for air. I tried in vain to control myself but I couldn't. Mum rushed out the car into a shop and got me a bottle of water and I took a Valium from my coat. I told her I didn't want it to knock me out and she said it wouldn't. I'd never had a tranquiliser in my life. I took the pill and eventually it started to work and I felt calmer. After about twenty minutes I continued driving to the hospital. In retrospect I was in no condition to drive but I wasn't thinking clearly. They had moved Dad to a private room. There had even been talk of moving him back to Barnet Hospital when a bed became available as apparently they had a better care plan and physiotherapy there. Dad was agitated. He was constantly trying to remove the bedcovers and was talking about going home. We repeatedly encouraged him to lay back down and I asked him if he would like me to read some psalms to him. His eyes were closed and he nodded and I opened my new book and started to read softly in Hebrew. I kept this up for a while and Dad seemed to relax and started breathing more easily. We stayed at the hospital late again. I can't remember who took Mum home that night but I remember getting into bed and lying awake throughout most of the night.

9

6th January 2016. My ex-wife had had the kids the night before (even though it was my night to have them). I had agreed to pick them up from her in the morning and take them to school before I went to the hospital. My alarm went off but I couldn't move. I forced myself out of bed. I didn't feel right and was starting to have a panic attack. It felt like I was falling down a deep dark hole. I couldn't breathe and was gasping for air – as though I was suffocating. I couldn't take a Valium as I would be unable to drive and get the kids to school. I made my way out to the car and tried to talk to myself and calm down. It wasn't working. I don't know how I didn't crash the car that morning on the way to get the children. I couldn't see properly and was shaking uncontrollably. I staggered up to the front door and rang the bell. She opened the door and I collapsed inside the house crying. I made my way to the kitchen and asked for some water. I took a Valium and stood there for ten minutes clutching onto the kitchen bench trying to calm down. I eventually sat down on the couch. She disappeared upstairs. I found out later than she had phoned my sister and told her I couldn't go to the hospital and that she would take the kids to school. I don't think my children saw me in that state which I'm thankful for. Eventually the kids appeared singing 'Happy Birthday' and giving me cards and presents. I had completely forgotten it was my birthday. By this time the pill was kicking in and I was feeling knocked out. I lay on the couch whilst my ex-wife took the kids to school and I think I spent most of the day there sleeping – I don't really remember. I felt very guilty for not being at the hospital but my mother and sister had said I wasn't to come. I just wanted to be with Dad and felt angry with myself for being in such a state.

That night I went home and had already decided that I would go to the hospital the next day against my family's wishes. One of my sisters was going to collect Mum the following morning so I drove straight to the hospital. When I arrived, as soon as I walked in the room, Dad seemed more alert and called me over and asked my mother to step outside as he wanted to have a private word with me. Mum went outside and I held Dad's hand and smiled down at him. It was clear that he couldn't remember what he had wanted to say to me and we chatted about nothing. This was going to be a very difficult day.

The nurses had been fitting feeding tubes through my father's nose to try and get some form of energy into him. At some point (most likely in a state of confusion) Dad had been pulling it out. The nurses wanted to try again but he didn't want them to. I begged him to let them and he smiled at me and agreed. All I can remember is gently stroking Dad's leg and Mum stroking the other leg as he kept asking them to stop. His legs were trembling and he had tears coming down his face. He was so weak and just kept saying 'Stop.' Eventually they finished the procedure and Dad wanted to blow his nose. The nurse held up a tissue but Dad smiled at me and said 'I want Daniel to hold the tissue.' I think he knew that I'd be really gentle. Or perhaps he wanted to let me know that he trusted me and had seen the look of horror on my face as I was trying to reassure him during the procedure and wanted to let me know he was ok. In any event, I look back now and it was the last act of kindness I was able to show him.

I had to leave the hospital by 2 pm in order to collect the children from school. The hospital had said that they were going to move Dad to a geriatric ward at some point during the night. Dad was asleep when I left. I kissed him gently and drove to my children's school in Barkingside. I parked in the car park and the panic started again. I got out my book of psalms and tried reading it but it wasn't working. I had to get out the car for some fresh air and tried a quick walk through the high street. I was feeling worse and worse. I eventually gave in and had a Valium and walked to the school playground.

I was in a daze and sat down on a bench outside my son's classroom. I think a few parents may have tried to talk to me but I couldn't focus. One of the assistants from my son's class took one look at me and brought me inside. I was in floods of tears but I eventually calmed down and drove the kids home. They asked the usual questions about their zeide. How is he? When is he coming home? 'I'm really not sure kids but he's in the best place until he's better and he sends his love.' I made the children their dinner and we probably watched some television until it was time for bed. Yaniv got into my bed – it was a habit I had been trying to break but I didn't have the energy to argue with him and I was glad of the company.

Chapter 2
Endings

1

My phone blasted out the James Bond theme. I woke with a fright. It was my parent's number. 5.25 am. I knew. 'Mum?' She sounded remarkably calm. 'Daddy stopped breathing at 5 am.' I tried to talk but no sound came out. My phone fell out of my hand to the floor and I quickly picked it up. 'Are you coming over?' 'Mum I have the kids here.' 'Ok I'll get a cab to the hospital.' 'No, I'll call their mother to come over and I'll get to you as soon as I can.' I called their mum. 'My dad's died. Please come straight over.' As much as those words were revolving around my head I knew I had to get to Mum as soon as I could.

I sat on the edge of the bed trembling. My son stirred and asked if I was ok. 'Yes darling, go back to sleep it's the middle of the night.' I quickly got dressed and went down-stairs. I stood in the dark waiting for her to arrive. At the time I didn't realise how long the wait was – she only lived ten minutes away. I later found out that she had left her car at the station that night and had had to catch a cab there to collect it and her car was frozen up. She eventually arrived. I asked her not to tell the children and just to tell them I'd had to go out early. I knew how devastated they would be and asked to stay at her place that night. In retrospect I shouldn't have asked but I knew I had to be there for the children and I also knew I shouldn't be alone. I got in the car and drove towards Southgate. I called both my sisters to see how they were doing. I must have been on autopilot as I drove. I arrived at my mother's house just before 7 am and opened the door. She was sitting at the table drinking a cup of coffee. I hugged her and cried. There was nothing we could say. She had phoned her sister Madeleine who was on her way round and was going to come to the hospital with us. I just wanted to get going but I sat down in Dad's chair and stared into space. My aunt turned up and gave me a hug. They both said that I wasn't to drive and we ordered a minicab which arrived fairly quickly. I remember the radio playing and my aunt asking the driver to turn the radio off as we had just suffered a family bereavement. The traffic was picking up at this point. I was starting to feel nauseous and wanted to ask the driver to pull over. I needed to get out, even for a few minutes but I needed to get to Dad and it took all of my strength to stay in the car and try to breathe slowly.

We arrived at the hospital and before we went inside, I quickly called my Rabbi, Nissan Wilson from Redbridge Shul to inform him. I was in a daze as we walked onto a different ward (they had transferred him during the night). Dad was in the end bed by the window. We went inside the curtain. Surely he was just sleeping? I stroked his hair and kissed his cheek. He felt so warm. I had been scared that he may have felt cold to the touch. I broke down and stood over him crying and thanked him for being my father. Mum was round the other side and checked that his arms were down his side in accordance with the Jewish burial practice. The nurses called me – there was a phone call. I went to answer. It was the hospital's Jewish chaplain. 'Sorry for your loss. You need to recite the first paragraph of the Shema and say Baruch Shem Kevod three times.' Sorry for your loss? Meaningless words. I wonder how many times he had recited that over the phone? I didn't have a siddur (Jewish prayer book) on me but fortunately I didn't need one. I stood over my father and looked down at him and recited the Shema whilst stroking his hair. Another phone call. It was Rabbi Yisroel Fine, the previous Rabbi of Cockfosters and North Southgate Shul. It was comforting to hear his voice. He'd known Dad very well and had just stepped off the plane from Israel. The nurses wanted to clean my father and I knew they were not allowed to. The Chevra Kadisha (the Jewish burial society) would prepare my father for burial in accordance with Jewish Law. Rabbi Fine told me they were not allowed to do anything to my father. The arguments started – as I'm sure happen on a daily basis all over the country. In the end we agreed to let them remove the feeding tube.

My sister Abigail arrived. Rabbi Fine had told me that I should cover my father's face with the bedsheet. I asked her if she wanted to see him and she nodded. I removed the sheet gently. I was very grateful to Emma's husband, Aviv, who turned up and had a bit of an eventful journey through London sorting out my father's death certificate. In the Jewish religion, burial needs to take place as soon after death as possible, which one cannot do without the death certificate. We sat next to my father. I was reciting psalms quietly as I believe my mother was. At some stage I went outside the hospital entrance to call Emma and check how she was. By the afternoon the hospital were ready to move my father's body to the mortuary.

As we were walking through the ward to the exit, a man (around the same age as me) who had been with a family member all day in the bed opposite, caught my eye and I stopped next to him. He hugged me with tears in his eyes. I have no idea who he was and assumed he was going, or about to go through the same ordeal. I hugged him back and to this day have no idea who he is but wish I could talk to him.

We had packed up Dad's belongings and accompanied him down in the lift and through some dark corridors. A body is not supposed to be left alone until the time of burial but these days due to health and safety laws we were unable to do that. I'll never forget my mother's words as they wheeled Dad into the mortuary. 'Bye Mark, thank you for everything'. My entire being was crying out to stay with him.

We walked slowly together to the hospital entrance where Abigail's husband, David, was picking us up. On the drive back to Mum's house we discussed where Dad should be buried – whether we should pick a particular plot or not. I didn't think it was necessary to have him in a particular place and knew that if he were to be buried in the new plot at Waltham Abbey Jewish Cemetery, that he would be close to our late cousin Alan Moss, who we had all loved very much. We all agreed with this.

We arrived back at Mum's place in the late afternoon. I was already dreading telling the children as I knew my sister was with her children too. We went through Dad's bag and I came across his kippah. I held it to my face and breathed in the smell and the tears came. My sister comforted me as best she could. I was trying my best to be strong for my mother and sister and not making a very good job of it. I've always been the emotional one unfortunately. Abigail was going through Dad's coat and found a rubber frog in his pocket. She asked our mother what it was doing there and she said that Dad had been feeling so ill and run down, but every time he put his hand in his pocket and held the frog there he was reminded of our planned trip to Israel for Pesach and how much he had been looking forward to spending time with his grandchildren. (Frogs are the second of ten plagues that were unleashed upon Egypt when the Pharoah refused to release the Jewish people from slavery).

I had discussed with Abigail the previous day about Dad wanting to have a private word with me. We came to the conclusion that he had wanted to tell me to look after our mother.

It was Friday night. Shabbat would be starting soon. I knew I had to get to my children. We couldn't stand the thought of Mum being alone and between Abigail, Auntie Madeleine and myself we managed to persuade her to get in the car on Shabbat to have dinner at Abigail's house. We hugged and cried and said our goodbyes and I got in my car and drove to my ex-wife's house.

I rang the doorbell and I went through to the lounge, sat on the couch and called the children. I knew I had to tell them immediately. I sat them next to me and I couldn't hold back the tears. 'Children, I'm really sorry, Zeide died this morning.' My eldest son Natan, jumped back as though he had received an electric shock. He burst into tears and ran up the stairs and flung himself on his mum's bed. I ran after him and did the best I could to console him. 'Zeide really wasn't well and he's no longer in pain and he loved you so much.' How much can you expect a nine-year-old to understand? My youngest son Yaniv who was six at the time had giggled nervously and then the tears came. I told them I would be staying over. We stayed there for a while comforting each other. I knew I had to go home to get some overnight things. I asked Yaniv if he wanted to come with me to keep me company. In truth, I needed his company more at that point. He said yes and we went to my place. We were only there for about ten minutes as I quickly threw some items into a bag.

Later on that night we made kiddush and I gave the children a blessing just as Dad had given me a blessing every Shabbat and Jewish holiday throughout my life. It suddenly dawned on me that I would never be receiving his blessing again or hear him speak and my voice choked up. I whispered to both my children that I loved them very much.

I was exhausted and wanted to sleep but did not want to be alone. We all went upstairs and climbed into bed – Yaniv next to me as usual. I was lying there with my eyes closed when suddenly my father's face descended next to me. It was as though he was starting to sit down on a chair next to the bed. He was looking down at the floor and his expression was sad. I noticed every single wrinkle and mark on his face. I turned to look and he wasn't there. 'Dad? Are you ok?' No answer. To this day I have no idea if I was asleep or if he really appeared. It was so real and I'm sure I was awake.

The next day we stayed at the house. In the afternoon we went to see some friends of mine. We chatted for several hours and I was glad to have got out for a while. When

Shabbat was over, I drove to Mum's place to meet with my sisters and try to come up with some sort of eulogy to give to Rabbi Fine to read out at the funeral the next day. I wasn't much help and my mother and sisters managed to piece something together, which I emailed over to him.

By this time the voicemails and text messages had started coming in. I wasn't in the right frame of mind to respond to any of them except to let people know the date and time of the funeral. I had deactivated my Facebook account a month earlier as I was getting tired of the messages coming in asking how Dad was doing. How can you respond to questions like that when you can't even accept the answer yourself? I had also grown more insular the worse my father got and had no interest in anyone else's life. On the drive home from Mum, I was wondering whether I should speak at the funeral. I didn't want to make a fool of myself but I knew Dad would have wanted me to say a few words. I decided to write a few things down, and see if I felt strong enough to speak when the time came.

2

Sunday 10th January 2016 (29th Tevet)

I set my alarm to go to shul. I had not attended on Friday night or Shabbat so felt I really should attend today. I hadn't slept well and switched off my alarm well before it was set to ring. I got my tefillin bag (phylacteries) – cubic black leather boxes with leather straps that Orthodox Jewish men wear on their head and their arm during weekday morning prayer, and drove to Redbridge Shul. I hadn't been involved with the shul for quite some time. I had attended regularly in the past to help out with making up a minyan (a group of at least ten men over the age of thirteen required for certain religious practices) for the evening service and had taken the boys occasionally on Shabbat but it must have been months since I had last attended. The usual people were there and I introduced myself to Rev Gary Newman who had continued in his duties when Newbury Park and Clayhall had merged and become Redbridge. I don't remember much about the service. I had my mind on the funeral. I also had this deep need to know that Dad had been properly looked after and prepared for burial in a respectful way but I had no way of knowing, which was significantly bothering me. I believe a friend of my sister went to Southgate Shul to collect Dad's tallit (prayer shawl) for him to be buried in. My brother-in-law, Aviv, had offered their house in Edgware for the shiva week, which I was very grateful for.

My ex-wife had arranged for a friend to look after the children and was going to drive me to the funeral. I was wondering whether to take my eldest son but I felt he wasn't old enough and I could remember that Dad hadn't let me or my sisters attend his mother's funeral when I was twelve.

We arrived early at Waltham Abbey Jewish Cemetery. Family and friends gradually started to turn up. Rabbi Epstein led us into the hall where my father's coffin had been placed and went through the service with us and according to tradition he made a rip in my jumper. Shortly after, Rabbi Fine entered with Rabbi Wilson – my Rabbi from Redbridge. I stared at the coffin. I was still numb. My dad, who had been so full of life, was inside that box. Rabbi Fine, who had known my father extremely well, was going to officiate. I told him I had prepared a few words but asked if he would mind checking with me when it was my time to speak, that I was ok to do so. The rest of the people started to file into the hall. I can't remember who was there but was grateful for the large turnout which showed a lot of respect to Dad.

I asked my brothers-in-law to stand either side of me. I looked across at my mother, who I had asked to remain seated throughout the service and was glad that my sisters were either side of her. The service commenced with the memorial prayers. I had attended many levayahs through-out my life, standing next to my father. It was hard to fathom that this was my own father's funeral. Rabbi Fine spoke beautifully and then it was my turn. He glanced at me and I nodded and went to the podium. I spoke for about five minutes. I mentioned some special times and memories and did my best to keep my voice steady. I'm not sure I suc-ceeded but I did it for Dad. We then reached the point that I had been dreading – the kaddish prayer. A beautiful prayer that sanctifies G-d's name. Contrary to popular belief, kad-dish is not a prayer for the dead. By sanctifying G-d's name and getting a group of ten or more men to respond to you – especially at a time of immense grief when one's belief in G-d may possibly waiver, brings tremendous benefit to the soul of the deceased. One is only allowed to recite the prayer with a minyan who responds to your prayers.

When I was twelve years of age, I witnessed Dad recite the kaddish prayer for his late mother Milly, our Grandma Malka, for eleven months when she passed away. He never missed one service. I had known even then that one day I would perform this mitzvah for my parents when the time came, but you can never be truly prepared. It was almost surreal. I tried to keep my voice loud so that everyone in the hall could respond. I just wanted to scream and leave the hall. 'Yitgadal V'yitkadash Shemei Rabba.' I was saying kaddish for my father. We had spoken about it over the years. I had always known how important it was for him to have kaddish said on his behalf. Apparently, one of the first things he had said to Mum when I was born was 'You have secured my kaddish.' I managed to get through it somehow.

Our father was then wheeled out of the hall towards the grave, with his family and friends following behind. We arrived at the grave and Rabbi Fine told me that the coffin would have to be tilted slightly when first being lowered to get it inside the foundation. I suppose he didn't want me to get a shock when we reached this point. The coffin was lowered and one side tilted quite sharply. I gasped and the words 'Daddy no' came from my mouth. Rabbi Fine put his arm around me with a tight grip. Dad had suffered throughout most of his adult life with arthritis. In that instant, I was worried that they may have hurt his neck when they tilted the coffin. The coffin levelled out and he was lowered the rest of the way. As the only son, I was told that I had to cover the coffin with the first three shovels of earth. I wasn't to hand the shovel to the next person but instead to put it back into the earth. I took the shovel and scooped up a big mound of earth and as delicately as possible, I sprinkled the earth around the side of the coffin. I couldn't bear to let the earth drop onto the actual coffin. I did the same with the second. For the third, I gently lowered the earth onto the middle of the coffin. If someone had to do it I would rather it was me. 'Sorry Dad, I hope that didn't scare you.' I placed the shovel into the earth and stood back. It was then my mother and sisters' turn. My mother remained behind us and shook her head when she was asked. She felt unable to move and couldn't bring herself to do it. My sisters were handed some mini shovels with some earth in a container. I couldn't look and stared at the ground. We stood watching the rest of the family and friends shovel the earth into the grave until it was full and we then walked back to the hall for the remainder of the service.

At the end of the service it is traditional for the mourners to sit down and everyone to line up and wish each mourner a 'long life'. However, due to the large amount of people there it was decided that all the family and friends would line up in a row and the mourners would walk up and down between them – an old tradition but more practical. I was relieved that I would have my mother and sisters next to me, but hadn't realised that there would be separate rows for the men and women, so whilst my mother and sisters were together, I had to do the walk by myself. Again, I kept my eyes to the ground and walked through the hall between all the males, really needing to be next to Mum and my sisters but unavoidably being separated from them. Finally we exited the hall and went to our cars. I don't remember who took me to my sister's house in Edgware, nor how I got home that night.

Emma lit a seven-day memorial candle. The four of us sitting shiva, each sat in a low chair and were served the traditional mourners' meal of a hard-boiled egg and a bagel – both round, symbolising the circle of life. Family and friends started to arrive. I was hoping nobody would talk to me (I just wanted to be left alone) but I found some of the conversations going on around me quite interesting and they distracted me from my own bleak thoughts. The Edgware community, Emma's friends, had organised a food rota and were sorting out dinner for us every night which we were very thankful for. It didn't occur to me at the time to thank them, or others for their acts of kindness. Emma's husband

Aviv, appeared often during the shiva week to make sure we were ok and frequently offered us hot drinks.

It was time for Mincha and Ma'ariv – the afternoon and evening prayers where I would recite kaddish again. More and more people started to turn up and my worries about getting a minyan soon dissipated. I didn't really want to lead the service that night but again, I knew Dad would have wanted me to. I stood at the front of the room by the memorial candle and led the services and recited the kaddish prayer at the end. Every night, a Rabbi would lead psalms of comfort following the service.

I was exhausted as I'm sure my mother and sisters were. As soon as people started to leave I left too. I was still staying with my ex-wife but don't recall how I got back that night. It was late and I must have gone to sleep shortly after.

3

Monday 11th January 2016. The shiva week.

The shiva (seven day mourning period) is the most intense time of mourning. A time of reflection, switching off from the outside world and concentrating on the memory of the deceased. A mourner is not supposed to do anything for themselves, no cooking, no bathing, etc. All mirrors in a house of mourning are covered. This symbolises that the use of the mirror is primarily for focussing on ourselves, and our external appearance. When we sit shiva we try to concentrate on the inner person who is no longer with us – not on the external appearance or possessions of the deceased.

My alarm went off at 5.30 am. I was already awake. I had decided that week to go to the Shacharit service at Southgate Shul and to then collect my mother and drive to Edgware. I left Chigwell at 6 am and arrived way too early at the shul. I let myself in and opened the door to the Beth Hamedresh. It was very dark. My father had loved this shul. He had been warden for many years and had still been actively involved until his ill health prevented him from attending. My thoughts went back to my childhood, sitting next to Dad in this room for all the services during his year of mourning when I was twelve and especially sitting next to him on Friday nights during the Kabbalat Shabbat service – Dad singing Lecha Dodi, slightly out of tune, slightly too loudly and slightly ahead of everyone else. I could really feel his presence in the room. I whispered 'morning Dad' in the dark.

I walked towards the main shul and entered through the doors. It felt strange being there in the darkness. I could remember standing on the bimah (a raised platform from where the service is led) with my dad so many years earlier practicing my barmitzvah. I wandered over to his seat and sat down. I placed my hands over the wooden book-holder in front of his seat and wondered when the last time was that he had sat here. Dad's tallit had already been collected for the funeral. I sat there in the dark, I don't know for how long, and wept. 'Please Dad, help me. Help me be strong enough to say kaddish for you. Don't let anyone turn up at shul and see me in this state.' I opened Dad's seat to see if anything was left in there and found a packet of disposable tissues. 'Thanks Dad.' I dried my eyes and headed back to the Beth Hamedresh. I put my hand in my coat pocket and felt Dad's frog. 'Come on Frog, you helped Dad stay positive for the future, please help me now.'

People were starting to turn up. I always loved the morning and evening services in any shul. The regular minyan attendees, who are the backbone to any shul community, are usually full of light-hearted conversation and jokes and lifelong friendships. I started to put on my tefillin. I was asked if I would like to lead the service. I just couldn't do it. I said no and remained at the back of the room. I found it very comforting seeing the same faces I had known since I was a small boy – people who had known Dad very well for many years. There are usually two types of kaddish which are said during the service by mourners – the Mourners' Kaddish and Kaddish D'Rabbanan which is usually recited after learning has taken place. Kaddish D'Rabbanan is longer and I used the siddur to read it. At the end of the service, a member of the community came to me and told me quietly that I had missed out a word at the end of Kaddish D'Rabbanan. I hadn't realised and was grateful that he had let me know and I went through it once more by myself to ensure that it did not happen again.

I drove to Mum. There was nowhere to park outside and I parked around the corner. I felt a huge sense of trepidation walking towards Mum's place. I hope she won't mind me mentioning that she has been plagued with various illnesses throughout her life – including depression (these days more commonly referred to as bipolar disorder). I was worried that losing Dad would push her over the edge and without him to keep an eye on her she may do something terrible. I was relieved to see the lights on through the net curtains and entered the house. Mum was at the table drinking her cup of coffee. I noticed she had also lit a memorial candle. I couldn't light one as I was too worried about leaving an open flame around my youngest son.

I had a cup of coffee and we left for my sister where the shiva was taking place. People turned up during the day and it was nice to have some visitors from Southgate shul and to reminisce about Dad.

I would get slightly worried leading up to the Mincha service and stare out the window until I knew that we had a minyan. Far more people would arrive for the evening prayers. I led the services again. Once people started to leave, I drove Mum home back to Southgate. I opened the front door and immediately felt a strange presence as we walked in. Mum felt it too. There was a sweet smell in the air and we both felt that we were not alone. I walked through the house in the dark calling Dad's name. 'Dad, are you ok?' I fully expected to find him there in the dark – perhaps trying to communicate with me. It's a feeling I can't explain and I'm glad Mum was with me and could feel and smell the same thing. I tried to put the smell down to the memorial candle but the next morning when I arrived after Shacharit, the smell was gone and the candle was still burning.

As I drank my coffee I was chatting with my mother, and mentioned that my knowledge regarding the customs of mourning were very limited. I was wondering about the different stages of mourning and various customs throughout the year that I may not be aware of. At the same time, and far more importantly – I needed to find out what was happening to my father's soul and the journey that he was now on. Although we were probably not supposed to, we agreed on the way to my sister that we would go into a Jewish bookshop in Edgware and see if there was any literature on the subject.

We entered the shop and browsed through the books. Finally we came across what I had wanted. *Mourning in Halachah* by Rabbi Chaim Binyamin Goldberg. We purchased it and got back in the car and drove to my sister.

I read the book as much as I could during the day and at night. It became almost like my bible in terms of observation and customs with some good explanations – but it did not have all of the information I needed to know. I had thought about death in the past but never like this. I needed someone, anyone, to explain what was now happening to my father's soul. Was he in heaven, was he still in this world, or in between worlds? Over the coming year I would find out the answers to the best of my ability.

4

Throughout the shiva week, to my relief, we had a good sized minyan at every Mincha and Ma'ariv service. Every evening we had a Rabbi in attendance from Southgate, Woodside Park, Edgware and Redbridge shul. At the end of the service, whichever Rabbi was officiating would give a talk and I hung on every word. Having not led a shul service for a while I was starting to get used to leading every service. Shacharit, Mincha and Ma'ariv. I have always been very nervous about public speaking or leading a service but it didn't seem to bother me anymore. I suppose I was still in shock at this point and feeling numb.

The days continued; Southgate Shul, collect Mum, head to Edgware, sit shiva, drop off Mum and head home. As tired as I was, I was taking so much comfort in having my mother and sisters with me. Looking back now, I think

Mum knew that she had to be strong for me and she was the most fantastic support and has been my constant rock right to this very day.

On the Wednesday, a close friend of my father came to see us sit shiva. We chatted for a while about Dad. I knew he was on the Chevra Kadisha – the burial society. It had been bothering me tremendously, that I did not know whether my father had been properly looked after and prepared for burial in strict accordance with Jewish Law. I decided to ask him. He started to get emotional and I suggested we went to the kitchen. He told me that in fact, it had been him who had looked after my father and he then proceeded to explain the full process of Tahara to me – preparing, cleaning and clothing the body for burial. He spoke kindly and with tenderness and it was clear to me that Dad had been treated with love, dignity and respect. I will always be grateful to him for reassuring me. We dried our eyes and went back to the shiva room.

On the Thursday we started to worry that the seven-day memorial candle was going to go out. Emma got another one ready and asked me to light it. I was very grateful to be asked as I had not lit one and really appreciated her thoughtfulness.

I found the last night of the shiva very hard to deal with. I had become accustomed to the days spent with my family and needed them around me. Even the visits from friends and relatives had been fine and had almost been a distraction from my thoughts. Emotionally I was feeling worse every day. The antidepressants were not helping. We finished the Ma'ariv service and once again the Rabbi spoke beautifully. Then my brother-in-law, David spoke. David had been the last person to visit Dad on the Thursday evening before he passed away. His death had hit him very hard and he spoke from the heart.

Once the visitors left, I drove Mum home again to Southgate. I hated leaving her in an empty house but I was becoming more exhausted every day and I knew Mum felt the same and just wanted to get into bed.

We were supposed to sit shiva on the Friday until we needed to start preparing for Shabbat. I don't recall there being any visitors on that day. At around midday we finished sitting shiva. I needed to drop Mum back home and get back to Chigwell and get ready for shul. I couldn't hold back the tears as I hugged my sisters. I dropped Mum back home and made sure she was ok. I was still staying with my ex-wife and children and went back there and showered (finally) and put my suit on. I was starting to worry about the Friday night service. When Kabbalat Shabbat begins, any mourners have to leave the service at this point and are not allowed to re-enter until after Lecha Dodi has been sung. I remembered only too clearly thirty years earlier, accompanying Dad to shul on the Friday night after our Grandma Malka died and seeing Dad leave the service. I had wanted to wait outside with him but he had told me I wasn't supposed to. I vividly recalled the tears in his eyes as he finally came back in and the congregation recited 'Hamakom y'na-chaym et-chem b'soch sh'or avay-lay tzi-yon virushlolyim' – 'May the Almighty comfort you amongst the mourners of Zion and Jerusalem.'

I was glad that I had been able to be with Dad on that horrible Friday night but was only too conscious that I was going to go through this alone. At nine years of age, I felt my son

Natan was too young and didn't want him getting any more upset than he had already been.

I arrived at shul and led the Mincha service. A mourner is not supposed to lead the service on a joyous occasion such as Shabbat or on a festival. Mincha finished and I recited kaddish and then as the congregation started to sing Yedid Nefesh, I left the service and sat by myself in the hall. I had never felt so alone in my entire life as I did at that moment. I thought about Dad and all the Friday nights in my childhood that I had sat next to him at Southgate Shul singing Yedid Nefesh and I looked out of the window hoping for a sign that he was ok and that he was still with me but I felt nothing. I began to weep and only tried to stop when the Shammas came and sat next to me.

Lecha Dodi was over and I made my way back into the service and was given the traditional greeting. It felt like a horrible dream that I prayed to wake up from. How could this be happening? I didn't make eye contact with anyone and made my way to the back of the hall and did my best to continue davening (praying), my mind not really on the prayers at all. I felt totally and utterly alone.

5

The next day I turned up at shul for 9 am as the first kaddish is said after approximately ten minutes. I know the layout of most of the services very well but had never really given much thought until this moment as to when all the kaddish prayers are recited and which ones. I checked through the siddur just to make sure I was prepared.

For approximately six weeks over the winter period, when Shabbat finishes so early, the congregation davens Mincha after kiddush following the morning service. This usually took place at 12.30 pm when I would finally go home until the end of Shabbat and would return again for Ma'ariv. I most likely went from there to check on my mother but I don't remember.

On the Sunday morning, I went to Redbridge shul for Shacharit. When I got back I had a chat with my ex-wife and she suggested it was time I went back home. I knew she was right. We didn't want to give the children false hope that I would be staying there permanently. She had been very kind to me in the weeks leading up to my father's passing and looking after the children so that I could be at the hospital. Truth be told, I was petrified of being alone. Petrified about the future – how I was going to survive and carry on with life. I needed to be around people to distract me from the loss of my father. Natan had taken his zeide's death particularly hard and I wanted to be with him every day.

I gathered my things and left the house. I didn't want to go home straight away and went to the shops to get a few items. Whilst I was there I bumped into some friends who had been Natan's childminders for several years. They had heard about my father and were very kind towards me. I was trying my best to act as though I was ok but when we said goodbye, I broke down. They both hugged me and we cried together. We must have looked a sight in the middle of a supermarket.

I drove home and opened the front door. I was trying to stay calm. The house was the same but I felt like a stranger entering a property for the first time. I put my shopping items away and sat down and looked around the lounge at my dvd and cd collection and the television staring at me. I gathered some bin bags and loaded all of the dvds and cds into them. I left the kids' one's there and put the bags in the loft. During the year of mourning one is supposed to abstain from listening to music, watching movies, attending celebrations, etc. It really boils down to the level of observance that one keeps. I decided that when the children were staying with me, I would allow the television to be on. It's not as though I got any particular joy from the CBeebies. My shul did not have a service on Sunday evenings so I decided to go to Chigwell & Hainault Shul for Mincha and Ma'ariv. I waited outside the doors with a few other people waiting for someone to open up. Rabbi Baruch Davis turned up and was surprised to see me. When I had first moved to the area I had been a member of this shul before I had joined Redbridge. I told the Rabbi I had lost my father and once again couldn't help the tears. He was very kind to me at that moment.

6

I knew that I would have to start sorting through Dad's estate. He had always been a very private man and had never discussed his financial situation with me. I knew that my parents had both saved carefully over the years, affording them to be able to live a comfortable life in their retirement. I was aware that several years earlier – my father's solicitor had retired and Dad had emailed me the details of his new solicitor for future reference. He had also sat me down about four years earlier and taken me through the contents of his will. I was astounded at the time at the level of thought my parents had put into this. One more thing I remembered from my childhood was that Dad had kept a black tin box above his wardrobe. He had always told me as a child, that should anything ever happen to him, I should give the box to his solicitor. This was really all the information I had to go on. I had no idea at the time the many months it would take me to sort through everything.

The following morning I took the black box down from the top of Dad's wardrobe and also took a copy of his will and placed them on the dining table next to Mum. I opened the black box wondering after all these years what I would find inside. I was perhaps hoping to find a letter addressed to me with his instructions. There was no such thing inside the box – it contained more personal items. He must have changed things around over the years. I briefly read through his will and it was as I remembered. I knew I had a daunting task ahead. I needed to find any assets and also find out what income my parents had been living off. My father was of the generation where he took care of everything and didn't explain much to my mother. I still wasn't in the right frame of mind to take matters any further at this stage and had to leave by 2 pm to pick up the boys from school.

The next morning, I needed to prepare my children for school and was agitated that I would not be able to get to shul to say kaddish. It was really playing on my mind and by the time I had dropped the boys off I was fixating on the fact that I had missed out on saying kaddish five times (on average one gets to recite kaddish five time at the morning service). In desperation I drove to Stamford Hill. I drove down the A10 past the Lubavitch building looking out for any shul – there was no shortage and then spent a while trying to find a parking space.

I walked across the road and entered the gates of a building. There were a lot of Chassidim outside chatting and drinking coffee from an urn. I approached them and asked if there was a Shacharit service inside. They were very friendly and first asked me to have a coffee with them, which I politely declined. I was in a bit of a state and feeling a bit shaky. They told me there were plenty of services going on and to just choose one. I entered the building. It was enormous and there were plenty of different rooms all with their own services going on – some really large and others smaller. I went inside one and started putting on my tefillin. It became clear to me that I couldn't follow the service and didn't have a clue where anyone was up to as the service was completely different to anything I was used to. In desperation I explained to some men that I was in mourning and needed to say kaddish and asked them to let me know when we were about to get to that point. They let me know in due course and I got to recite it and felt slight relief. I didn't stay for too long after and davened by myself. I felt like a fish out of water and realised I couldn't do this every day. Somewhat despondent, I made my way to my car and drove to Southgate to Mum's place.

7

I spoke with my mother, regarding my concerns that I was not going to be able to go to Shacharit on the mornings I had the boys as I needed to get them up and ready for school and told her about my rather hectic morning. She knew how much this was bothering me and offered to stay at my place as much as possible to help out. I was really grateful for this offer – I hoped she had enough strength to be able to manage the children but it also meant that

I would get to spend more time with her and I gratefully accepted her offer.

Mum always prepared a lovely lunch for me when I was there – really simple but presented so nicely; a sandwich and salad and she had even peeled and laid out an orange for me, just how she had done for Dad. I found this really comforting. Mum also makes a bean and barley soup, which I had never been particularly fond of and used to teasingly refer to it as her 'gruel' but it suddenly became the most comforting meal to me.

Mum would stay with me on Monday and Tuesday nights and get the boys up and ready for school whilst I was at shul. I always did my best to make her as welcome as possible and tried to plan nice meals we could have together. Mum is a vegetarian so I always planned accordingly. I usually took one or both the boys to the Mincha/Ma'ariv service with me. It only lasted twenty minutes and I felt it was important for them to witness me saying kaddish for their zeide as I had witnessed my father do for our grandma, and as I hoped they would do for me when my time came. I also reflected on the fact that as Dad had been an only child, I was the only son, so reciting kaddish was my responsibility. The Chief Rabbi had recently declared that it was quite acceptable for a woman to recite kaddish. Each to their own but it was not something I felt Dad would have been comfortable with, nor was I, and I don't think my sisters were. I realised how lucky my sons and nephews, Jonah and Gabriel, are to have each other and that when the time comes, they would hopefully stand side by side in shul to support each other and to arrange to say kaddish between themselves. That is my wish anyway.

The next morning I left for shul. Upon arriving home I found the boys awake and dressed and sitting at the table with Mum having breakfast. I was delighted at Mum's help and how she seemed to have a newfound strength.

Another problem I faced was that as we were in the middle of winter, most shul's could not hold an afternoon service, as it got dark so early. I needed to find services I could attend for Mincha. When I was local I could go to Chabad in Gants Hill but I had no idea where I could go when I was in Southgate as apart from on a Wednesday, Southgate did not hold a Mincha service in the winter months during the week. Luckily, Abigail found out that Barnet Shul held an afternoon service every day. It was only an eight minute drive from my mother's place and I was relieved to have found somewhere to go. The shul had a very welcoming atmosphere and were always respectful of the fact I was in mourning and were only too happy to allow me to lead the service on the days that none of their members had yahrzeit.

I placed a call to my father's solicitor and informed her of his passing. I was not very impressed with her response. I found her attitude to be very cold-hearted and uncaring and decided not to use them. On my cousin's advice I secured the services of a solicitor in Southgate. I also called a very trusted friend of my father who was able to give me lots of practical advice. It was clear to me throughout our conversation that Dad had discussed his finances with him over the years and I fully trusted his advice, as Dad had.

My father had been a very organised man, which I was thankful for. He kept a filing cabinet in the office and I decided the best place to start would be to go through everything. I was still hoping that Dad may have left a letter in the filing cabinet addressed to me but there was nothing there.

8

Approximately two weeks after my father passed away, there was another tragedy in the local community. A mother of one of the children in my son's year at school had been fighting cancer for a number of years and finally passed away. I had got to know the family quite well over the past few years. Kay Cohen was a very special person who was well loved by all who knew her. She was selfless and had a knack of steering any conversation away from herself and truly cared about others. As I got to know her, we came to confide in each other and she helped me in many ways throughout my divorce. I had always completely trusted her – a rarity for me.

Kay was only thirty-seven years old when she passed away, leaving behind her wonderful husband Spencer, daughter Mia, and son Zak. She once told me of a time Mia, who is the same age as Natan, told her that she knew she wasn't going to be around for much longer. Kay couldn't deny this fact and just held her really tight and told Mia that when she was no longer around to remember that hug always. That conversation has always stuck in my mind.

We knew that Kay did not have much time left, but the shock of her passing was felt by everyone in the community. I knew I wasn't strong enough to go back to Waltham Abbey Cemetery so soon after my father's burial but I felt I had to go.

I arrived at the cemetery early and walked towards my father's grave – a mound of earth with a marker. One is not supposed to say prayers over the grave until after the stone setting and is also not supposed to ask anything of the deceased during the first year as they are in their own period of reflection. I could not believe that my father was buried just where I was standing. It felt surreal. Still in a bit of a daze I walked back to the hall. The cemetery was filling up with all of Kay's family and friends. I have never seen such a crowd of people ever at a levayah. I stood closely with some friends from the school until we went into the hall for the service.

Following the memorial prayers, it was time to accompany Kay to her final resting place. We walked behind the coffin, in the same direction as my father. Hundreds of people were walking past my father's grave, not having the slightest idea that he had only been buried there two weeks earlier. I felt physically sick and hung back at the burial.

As people started to gradually head back towards the hall for the conclusion of the service, I felt unable to join them and walked slowly towards the car park. In retrospect I shouldn't have gone. It was far too soon but I'm glad I was able to show my respects to Kay and her family.

Kay (Chana Malka) is buried just around the corner from my father and I always visit and say a few prayers whenever I go.

9

The days continued in much the same way. Shacharit at 7 am followed by spending the rest of the morning at Mum's sorting through piles of paperwork. Then, depending on what day it was, either leaving to pick up the children from school or staying at Mum a little later.

The children had been staying at my house on Monday, Tuesday and Friday nights. I swapped Friday for Saturday nights, so that I could go to shul on Friday evenings and Shabbat. I now had the children on Sundays, which was the only morning of the week that I could not attend the Shacharit service, therefore, I ensured that I could attend the Mincha and Ma'ariv services on that day.

I did my best during this time to continue to gradually sort through all the paperwork including submitting the online GOV form – notifying the relevant authorities of Dad's passing. I came across some paperwork from a financial advisor my father had used in the past. After I spoke with them, I understood that he had not used their services since 1997, which was around the same time he had retired and I assumed he had decided to manage his financial affairs by himself.

We made some slight changes to Mum's house. Nothing extreme – just to get things more to her liking. We turned the office into a second bedroom. I got rid of some very old bookcases and we adjusted the furniture in the lounge and made changes to the bedroom. I recalled asking Dad in hospital if there were any bills that needed paying. He told me that most of them were on direct debit and that it was fine. Clearly, at this stage Dad was intending on coming home.

I had to close all of Dad's credit cards and accounts that were in his name and re-open accounts just for my mother. Each time I had to email or post off a death certificate it was devastating. Still to this day, when letters arrive at my house addressed 'To the executor of Mark Rose, deceased' my heart jumps.

The more time that passed, the more questions I needed to ask my father. Why did you keep this account open with Barclaycard? Would you prefer Mum to pay her credit card in instalments or in one go? Do you mind me saying kaddish for you at Chabad as it is recited in a different way? Slowly, as I pieced everything together those questions became unimportant. All I wish now is that I could hug my dad just one more time and tell him how much I love him.

It was around this time that Mum spoke to me about Pesach. We had agreed together to cancel the trip to Israel shortly before my father had passed away. I had promised Mum that whatever happened we would still be together for the seder nights. Mum wanted to re-book Israel saying the trip had already been paid for and it was what Dad would have wanted and she still wanted the family to be together at this time. I was really not comfortable with this. How could I even think about going away when I needed to say kaddish? I told Mum that Dad would never have gone away during his year of mourning and that I couldn't go. Over the next few days Mum got more insistent that we were going to go. I kept holding out – I admired her determination but it was not something I felt I could do. I finally gave in on the condition that the family would help out with looking after my children so that I could still go to shul. Everyone agreed and Mum phoned the travel agent and re-booked the trip.

Rabbi Epstein from Southgate Shul contacted me. He had been thinking about having a siyum (the completion of any unit of Torah study, or book of the Mishnah or Talmud) at the shul to mark the end of my father's Shloshim (the first thirty days of mourning). He proposed that we take on the learning of Talmudic Tractate 'Mo'ed Katan'. The completion of a single tractate is what enables a formal siyum to take place. I thought this was such a wonderful suggestion and a huge honour for my father. I agreed immediately and contacted family members and friends to inform them of the date and the shul sent out a notification to the wider community. We decided between ourselves who would learn what and I was happy to know that Rabbi Fine would also be involved and would be speaking on the day.

As I started to learn the tractate, I realised why Rabbi Epstein had chosen Mo'ed Katan as it deals with the subject of death and burial. I became fascinated by what I was reading. My father had a set of Talmud on his bookshelf in the office. He had enjoyed collecting them when he attended group study sessions with Rabbi Fine. He did not have Mo'ed Katan in his collection so I made a trip with Mum to Torah Treasures in Golders Green to get my own copy. Whilst we were there I asked on the off chance if they had any books covering the subject of death from a Jewish perspective. The lady walked towards the front of the shop and bent down to a lower bookshelf and handed me a book called *Soul Searching* by Yaakov Astor. We thanked her and paid and headed back to Mum's.

It was this book that held the answer to so many questions I had. It made me reflect on the subject of death from a completely different perspective. I realised that heaven or the World to Come is not up in the sky but most likely through another dimension. It also got me thinking that how we live our lives in this world is a test and we will receive our rewards in the World to Come. Just as importantly, I understood that our Nefesh (our soul) is our being. Not the brain or the heart. In this world, our body is simply a vessel to carry our soul. When the body ages or the body shuts down, the soul departs the body and continues to exist – no longer confined to the needs of oxygen, food and material possessions. I could go on about this subject for pages and pages but am not trying to change anyone's views on the subject of life after death but am stating my own belief. The soul departs the body and starts a new journey – a journey of reflection that almost mirrors the journey of the mourners who have been left behind. The subject of death does not scare me. I know that when my time comes, my father will be waiting for me as his father Louis, was waiting for him after sixty years.

It was this book that also led me to be fascinated by Near Death Experiences (NDEs) and the possibility of reincarnation. I started downloading books to my kindle and reading any scientific literature on the subject that I could get hold of. I was particularly interested in NDEs experienced by young children. Too young to have had any previous knowledge on the subject but nearly all the NDEs described were remarkably similar. Again, I am not going to describe these experiences but would recommend to anybody who is interested or feels the need to know more on the subject, to read *Many Lives, Many Masters* by Brian Weiss.

10

I was staying in close contact with my sisters. We spoke on the phone and I saw them most days when they came in to visit Mum. They were obviously going through their own stages of grief and doing their best to manage during these difficult times. Abigail started to frequently invite me to stay with them on Friday nights.

If I couldn't be with my own children, then being with my nephews was the next best thing. David would accompany me to Woodside Park Shul on Friday nights. After the service there was plenty of good quality whisky on offer. I had never been much of a whisky drinker but was starting to enjoy my weekly shots. As we walked home, David and I used to chat about anything and everything. One of the first times we walked home together I asked him if Dad had talked about anything in particular on the Thursday evening when David had visited. I found great comfort in being at their house – a lovely, warm Friday night atmosphere, a traditional Friday night dinner and having lots of hugs with my nephews.

By the time dinner was over, I was so exhausted that I used to excuse myself and go straight to bed. Sometimes before the children had gone up.

On Shabbat mornings I would leave for shul to be there for the start and later on David would arrive with the children. During this time, like with my shul, Mincha was directly after kiddush and I then made my way back to their house for lunch. Abigail and David would usually like to take the boys for a walk to the park in the afternoon where a lot of the local families would meet up. I accompanied them on several occasions but most of the time I had to ask them if they minded if I didn't come and had a nap instead.

I felt bad for sleeping so much but I was desperately tired – suffering from constant exhaustion and I knew they wouldn't mind. When I woke up I would go back to shul after Shabbat for Ma'ariv and then drive home.

Chapter 3
Grief

1

I was feeling increasingly run down and depressed. On the days and nights that I had my boys I at least had a distraction from my grief. On the nights that I was alone, life was unbearable. Looking back now, I was suicidal. I would never have acted on this. I could never deliberately leave my children without a dad or have my mother sit shiva for me. However, I used to go to bed at night and pray that I would not wake up in the morning. All I wanted was to be with my father. Some nights were worse than others. The best I could hope for was not to be a sobbing mess – suffering panic attacks that were becoming increasingly severe. I could not take joy in anything – even in my own children. I recall one morning driving to Southgate shul at approximately 6.20 am. The panic was rising and I was trying hard to fight off my depths of despair. My driving was becoming erratic and I was thankful there were not many others cars on the road at that time of the morning. I drove past the road to the shul and straight to my mother's house and double-parked outside. I knew the chain would be on and I unlocked and opened the door and called to her through the gap. I didn't want to startle her but I was in a terrible state. She rushed to the door and took the chain off. I went inside, through to the kitchen, and took a Valium trying to catch my breath. Mum sat there with me in silence. I knew she was desperately worried about me but I couldn't talk and was sobbing uncontrollably. I started to calm down after ten minutes and left the house to get to shul in time for Shacharit.

My exhausted state was not getting any better and it was becoming a more frequent occurrence that I would try and take a quick nap during the day but when I managed to actually sleep, I would wake up feeling even more tired.

My father's seventy-eighth birthday would have been on February 5th. It was a difficult day for all of us. Abigail sent us a lovely message describing Dad's day in heaven with his parents and departed loved ones. Her accurate description of our beloved family members interacting together was fantastic. Every year I eagerly anticipate her annual message describing what Dad is doing on his birthday.

The end of my father's Shloshim was on February 7th and we arrived at Southgate Shul in the afternoon. We would be commencing with the Mincha service, followed by the siyum upstairs in the hall, which would include a talk from myself, my brother in law Aviv, Rabbi Fine, and also some members of the community who were close with my father. We would finish with Ma'ariv downstairs again in the main shul. I was stunned at the turnout. There were so many people and it once again showed how respected Dad had been in the community he had been a part of for forty-six years. I was feeling increasingly nervous. Rabbi Epstein came into the main shul and gave me a hug, which instantly made me feel less isolated. I was also really pleased that my

Rabbi, Rabbi Wilson, was in attendance as well as so many members of our family.

I led the Mincha service and we went upstairs to the hall, which had been laid out beautifully by the Ladies Guild.

Rabbi Epstein opened the proceedings and then invited me to speak. I used the opportunity to mention how much my father had loved the shul and how much comfort I was getting on being able to attend the Shacharit service there amongst the same faces I had known since I was a small child. I also thanked my family for their love and support.

Aviv spoke very warmly about my father and really moved me with his kind words. Rabbi Fine did the same and spoke about Dad with great affection.

It was then time to finish the Tractate of the Talmud. I had made some notes and shared some of my findings with everyone in the room. Upon finishing I had to recite Kaddish De'itchadata – a kaddish that is only recited on very rare occasions, one of them being upon completion of a tractate. The beginning paragraph is quite long and the words are difficult to pronounce but I managed to get through it. We then went downstairs to the main shul for the Ma'ariv service. Rabbi Epstein once again did something very kind. He took his tallit and wrapped it around my shoulders and said I deserved to wear it to lead the service. I was feeling overwhelmed at how the evening had gone and as I led the service I could really feel my father's presence next to me.

I knew Dad would have been so proud of his family and the community. I was exhausted and after dropping Mum home I left for my house. Later on that evening I received a lovely message from Abigail telling me how proud she was. It meant the world to me and despite the sorrow, I realised how lucky I was to have such a loving family around me.

2

During the shiva week we had discussed when to hold our father's stone setting and had decided on Sunday 13th November 2016. I had an idea of what type of memorial stone I wanted to get and discussed it with Mum. I had come across several invoices in Dad's filing cabinet to Elfe's in Edgware and we drove there. We went through various designs and sizes. We wanted something traditional and in the end we went for a black, double headstone with a slight curve at the top and we also chose a memorial plaque from the grandchildren. I initially wanted to have a gold plated inscription but Abigail felt that silver was smarter and we agreed with her. It must have taken me months to get the wording how I wanted it.

Traditionally, if you look at headstones in a Jewish Cemetery, the inscription starts with the Hebrew letters Peh and Nun. These letters represent either the phrase 'Po Nikbar or 'Po Nitman' which simply mean 'Here Lies'. However, on my grandparents' headstone (which Dad had updated in 1986 when his mother passed away) was the word L'Zichron, (in memory of). I thought this phrase was a lot nicer and decided to have that on Dad's stone instead of 'Peh Nun'.

This is then followed by the Hebrew name and the Jewish date on which Dad passed away. I checked the date so many times to ensure I got it correct. We then had the English inscription underneath and chose two Magen David's (Stars of David) to go either side of the stone at the top.

Because we had chosen a double stone I had to ask the awkward question as to what the process would be when we needed to fill in the bottom part of the stone. Mum has always been very practical and did not mind me asking – in fact I was far more bothered about the question than she was.

It is also traditional to have the following abbreviations placed at the bottom of the inscription. – 'ת' נ' צ' ב' ה *תהא נפשו צרורה בצרור החיים* – may his soul be bound up in the bond of everlasting life. I wondered for a long time what these words actually meant and many months later I was given an explanation. There are five parts to the soul – which range from the most spiritual – the Chaya and Yechida to the Nefesh – the life force of the body. My father – his Neshama – is now on a greater journey in heaven but a part of his soul remains with us and as long as he stays in our thoughts and our hearts we can always do good deeds to his merit. Therefore, his soul is bound up in the bond of everlasting life in the World to Come as well as very much here with us.

We paid the deposit, glad that we had got a very difficult job out of the way.

I continued to sort through Dad's estate. The process was taking far longer than I had anticipated. I wasn't in any rush and worked around my shul commitments and the children. One thing I was glad I had done so quickly was get myself added to Mum's bank accounts. It became easy to keep an eye on any unusual transactions and I also had alerts set up on her bank accounts and credit cards so that if there was any unusual activity I would receive an instant alert to my phone. This has only happened once. It was a very unfortunate situation that I don't want to go into, but I was glad I received the alert and was able to immediately act. I was continuing to sort through Dad's filing cabinet and although I was initially reluctant, I began to shred documents and receipts that we would never need. I set up three separate folders with document I wanted to hang on to.

Shul – Dad had been Gabbai (Warden) of his shul for many years and had been as involved in later years as his health allowed. He had organised the call ups with much thought and care and I couldn't stand to throw away any of these documents.

Medical – Dad had unfortunately had many medical ailments over the years and again I set up a file with all of these documents should any of us ever need to reference them.

Personal – Letters and documents received over the years that Dad had held onto that again I couldn't stand to throw.

The main filing cabinet I continued to use under the same index system that Dad has set up but mainly with documents that Mum would need going forwards.

I was slowly building up an accurate picture of my mother's income, savings and investments. Finally, when I felt I had done all that I could, I handed all documentation over to the solicitor to arrange transfer into Mum's name. The process took months and months. I had paid off any outstanding bills on Dad's credit cards – he didn't owe anyone any debt. I set up as many utility bills as I could under direct debit so that Mum didn't need to worry about this.

I was still upset that Dad had never left any final instructions – his estate was like a huge jigsaw puzzle. I decided that I didn't want to leave anyone else in that situation and as I pieced everything together, I wrote everything down so that should anything ever happen to me, my sisters would have all the information they needed to look after Mum's financial wellbeing. I tried on many occasions to explain Mum's financial situation to her, but she had spent so many years having Dad take care of everything that she didn't want to start having to change. She used to say as long as I said she was fine financially then that was good enough for her. It doesn't bother me and if she prefers things this way then I am more than happy – especially now that the hard work is over.

I found Friday nights at shul to be the hardest night of the week emotionally. In any shul, you get a warm welcoming atmosphere and I used to love attending the Friday night service with Dad. Whenever the Kabbalat Shabbat service commenced, it would just drive home the fact that Dad was no longer with us. It was the time when I felt most isolated from everything and everyone. I would sit at the back of the service doing my best to fight away the tears. Sometimes I succeeded – usually I didn't.

I knew that Abigail was becoming increasingly worried about me. She used to say my eyes were dead and persuaded me to go to a private psychiatrist. She drove me there and I had an hour's session. We spoke mainly about how I was coping (or not coping). At the end of the session he called my sister in and told her that I was grieving. I was going through a natural process and it will last as long as it lasts – it may take years but in time I would be ok. I came out, not really feeling any better. I had not given any thought at the time as to who was paying for the session. A few weeks later an invoice arrived at my house. My sister had instructed them that she would settle the bill but they had accidentally sent it to my address. When I opened it and saw the amount I was shocked. I called my sister and she was very annoyed that I had seen it. The psychiatrist may not have been able to help me, but when I saw the amount Abigail and David were happy to spend on me out of love and concern, I felt so incredibly lucky to have the family that I do.

3

I don't usually remember my dreams. I can sometimes wake up in a sweat after a particularly nasty dream where I can remember some fragments but in general I don't remember. However, one dream I had was so incredibly vivid.

I was in the Beth Hamedresh at Southgate Shul and I was leading the morning service. I turned around at one point and my father was standing there praying. I didn't know what to do. I remember worrying about whether I should go over and talk to him or leave him alone to pray. I walked over to him and said 'Dad are you ok?' He smiled and nodded at me. Should I let him know that he had died or would that worry him? He then looked at me and said, 'Check the lights.' I didn't know what he meant and felt confused. I asked him if he knew what had happened to him. I couldn't bear to say the word 'die'. He looked me straight in the eye and smiled at me – the warmest and gentlest of smiles. It was at this point I woke up. I stayed awake for the rest of the night wondering if it was a dream or if Dad had just wanted to let me know he was ok.

The next day I was at my mother's place. I hadn't mentioned the dream when she suddenly pointed at the wall and said, 'Oh the lightbulb's gone'. I went pale and told Mum about the dream. Dad had always immediately changed any lightbulbs the minute they went. I changed the bulb and felt warm inside. To this day I'm convinced that Dad just wanted to let me know he was ok and was still with me.

4

I had begun to scan and collate every photo I could find of Dad into the computer. Slowly but surely, I would take an album from Mum's house, carefully remove every photo (not always easy with the sticky backing) scan it into the computer and place each photo back into the album and repeat the process with the next album. I saw how the photos had deteriorated over the years, covered in scratches and the colour faded and I began the painstaking process of doing my best to restore every picture – blending out the scratches and trying to balance the colour, or, with the older pictures just trying to erase the scratches. It could take me hours just to finish one photo. It became almost an obsession but I concluded that if I didn't do it then these photos would be lost to future generations.

It was an act of love but probably not the healthiest of things I could be doing. I would continue with this project late at night when I couldn't sleep or on the evenings when I didn't have the children. At least I had something to occupy my time. I did the same with my parents' wedding album.

As I went through the pictures, I realised how little I knew of my grandfather Louis' side of the family – the Roses.

When we were growing up, Dad's mother's side of the family (the Briskis) were the family that we had known. I had on occasion over the years asked Dad why we had nothing to do with his father's side of the family. He never wanted to talk about it and to this day I have no idea what his reasons were. Both my paternal grandparents were one of ten brothers and sisters. Apart from knowing the names from a census, and the location of where his Uncle Reuben is buried at Marlow Road cemetery, I have no information to go on. I must have plenty of cousins on the Rose side of the family who I have absolutely no knowledge of. I spoke with Mum about it. I really wanted to find out what had happened. Grandpa Louis (who I am named after) had passed away suddenly when Dad was only seventeen years of age. It had been such a long time since then for me to suddenly start asking questions again. Most of the Briski family would not have any information as to what may have happened. Mum suggested that we call Dad's first cousin, Frances Rinder (grandmother of Robert Rinder – who has become a bit of a celebrity through his Judge Rinder television show). Apparently they had been very close when Dad was growing up. From what I could gather, she had been a bit of a big sister to him. Mum called but nothing really came of the conversation and we never did meet up for a chat. I suppose I may well never know.

Mum bought herself a digital photo frame. As I finished scanning and editing the pictures I would download them onto a memory card along with the latest pictures of the family and her grandchildren and leave the memory card in the frame. I believe there are over 4000 pictures to this day and it gives her a lot of pleasure.

5

We were coming to the end of February. I noted that my father's barmitzvah sidrah (Tetzaveh) was coming up. He had always leyened the first part in shul on Mondays and Thursdays whilst he was in good health. When I was fifteen years of age, I had been approached by Cockfosters' Shul (a satellite service held in Cockfosters) to help out with their leyening on Shabbat. I agreed and usually learnt a new sidrah between every six weeks to two months. Dad took great pride in hearing me leyen and would always accompany me there. I did this probably for a few years. Did I enjoy it? Not at all. I have always had a fear of speaking in public and learning an entire sidrah where the pronunciation of every word needs to be one hundred percent accurate. This used to fill me with dread. I had to put in a lot of time and effort – it does not come naturally to me. Then came a time, after I had spent a few months learning a new sidrah, that as I stood at the bimah at Cockfosters Shul, my mind went blank from start to finish. It was a nightmare. After spending so long making sure I knew it perfectly, I had to be prompted the entire way through. It was then that I decided never to leyen again. My father was very disappointed but I had made up my mind. Mum was far more understanding and agreed that I should not put myself through this trauma.

It must have been twenty-five years since I had last read from the Torah but I decided that I would like to start again and I would like to leyen the first part of Tetzaveh on behalf of my father. I spoke to my Rabbi who was only too happy for me to do it. I got the tikkun out again after all these years and started practising. I could hear Dad's voice in my head singing along too. The night before I leyened I told my Rabbi that it was my father's sidrah.

I was slightly nervous the next morning but I led the service as usual and took the Torah out of the ark. The first person was called up and I started to leyen. Miraculously, my nerves vanished and I was able to read it perfectly. I was really hoping that Dad had heard me and was feeling proud. At the end of the service, Rabbi Wilson always gave a D'var Torah which was followed by Kaddish D'Rabbanan. He mentioned how nicely I had leyened and also that it was my father's sidrah.

He then mentioned something that I will never forget. He said that everything I was doing was to my dear father's merit. It was at this moment that I realised that besides saying the kaddish prayer at every opportunity, there were other things my sisters and I could do to help our father and for our father still to take pride in. We were about to recite kaddish and once again I was unsuccessfully fighting back the tears.

I was also fortunate to leyen from the Torah again on the Thursday morning at Southgate shul. After this day, Rabbi Wilson often asked me to help out with leyening on the days he could not attend the service and after all these years I was learning new Torah portions to leyen again on a regular basis and having no nerves on the day. I know my father was well aware of how nervous I had been in the past and it almost felt as if he was calming me down.

6

My Grandfather Alf's Yahrzeit (the anniversary of the date of passing on the Jewish calendar) was approaching – Mum's father. It was very soon after my father's funeral but

I knew she would want to pay her respects. I offered to take her to Waltham Abbey and she invited her sister Madeleine to join us.

We arrived at the cemetery and headed towards their parents' grave, stopping at Madeleine's late husbands' graves along the way. I recited the memorial prayer. We then decided to walk to the other side of the cemetery to pay our respects to our late cousin Alan. Alan is buried on the plot before my father.

I knew I had to see my father's grave and felt myself tearing up. Even though one is not allowed to recite prayers I needed to stop by. I was worried about the effect this may have on my mother and I asked her to walk to the car with Madeleine and that I would join them soon.

I walked towards my father's grave and gazed down. I whispered hello and told him how much I loved him and missed him and stood there for a few minutes and slowly backed away and walked towards the car trying to compose myself. I was lost in my own world driving home.

Three days later it was my Grandfather Louis' yahrzeit. Dad had never missed visiting his parents' grave for a yahrzeit or during the Hebrew month of Elul. I had accompanied him many times. About seven years earlier, Dad had taken me around all the cemeteries pointing out the graves of departed family members. Having had no siblings, I decided it was incumbent upon me to keep my father's parents' memories alive by continuing to visit their grave and to recite kaddish on their yahrzeits. I have also continued to do this for my mother's parents and for her cousin Alan.

Whenever I accompanied my parents on cemetery visits, Dad always came armed with cleaning products and also a gold marker pen so that he could fill in any of the gold inscription that may have started to fade on his parent's gravestone. He had had it professionally maintained a few years earlier.

I drove through the gates at Marlow Road cemetery in the East End. Memories came flooding back. Dad had always visited his parents and then walked up to the corner of the cemetery to visit his late Uncle Reuben Rose – His father Louis' brother. Dad had always let me drive his car behind him as he walked to the corner of the cemetery – years before I took any driving lessons. I have the fondest memories of my Grandma Malka. She had passed away six months before my barmitzvah. She was the most fantastic cook – traditional haimishe cooking at its best. As she had tragically lost her husband so early (when Dad was only seventeen) she devoted all her time and love to Dad and then to her daughter-in-law and three grandchildren.

I parked where Dad had always parked the car and walked towards their graves, the gravel crunching under my feet. This was one of the first times I had made this walk without Dad next to me. Marlow Road first opened in 1919. I don't believe many burials take place there any more but the site still has a caretaker and is looked after. A lot of the headstones have been damaged or collapsed over time and it is always with a feeling of trepidation when I walk towards my grandparents' graves until I can see that the headstone is still in good condition.

I stood at the grave and read the inscription. Grandpa Louis had passed away in 1955 – sixty-one years ago. I knew how much my father had loved him. He had told me many stories about him including describing the night that he had died. Dad had told me that not one day had passed where he had not thought about him. He had also told me that he had had to go out and buy a new suit for his father's funeral – the last thing he had wanted to do but his mother had made him. All these thoughts passed through my head and I felt a sense of peace standing there, probably the only person in the cemetery as I asked my grandparents to look after my father.

A few days before Dad had passed away, Mum told me that he had been calling his father over and over again in a state of unconsciousness. I truly believed that Grandpa Louis has been waiting for Dad and that he had felt peaceful because of this and calmly accepted his journey into the next world. I also knew that Dad would be waiting for me when my time came.

I recited the memorial prayer and said a few psalms and proceeded to clean the headstone and remove a few weeds. It is traditional to leave a stone on the headstone as a mark of respect and to show that the loved ones are still remembered. I sorted out the stones that were already in place, left in the past by Mum, Dad and other members of the family and then chose three extra stones and placed them neatly next to the others. From Dad, Mum and myself.

I then walked over to Great Uncle Reuben as Dad had always done (he had passed away in 1953) and recited the memorial prayer again and placed another stone next to the others.

7

I hadn't had a haircut or shaved for two months. I had no interest in my appearance and wasn't planning on shaving my beard for the foreseeable future. My mother was starting to comment more frequently on my unkempt appearance and telling me every day to have a shave. I read that one should only shave when friends or family members start to comment. As this seemed to be causing distress to her I shaved my beard shortly after. Looking back at some photos that were taken during this period I suppose I was looking very scruffy!

It was coming up to Purim. I could hear Dad's words in my head. 'If I'm not well enough, I want you to use my megillah scroll on Purim.' Southgate Shul were having a 'wild west' themed night and I spoke with my sisters and we agreed to go to Southgate Shul that year.

I left with the children in plenty of time to collect Mum and get to shul. I had a look at Dad's megillah scroll and was amazed at how clear the writing was. We got to shul in time for the Mincha service, which was followed by the megillah reading. Despite a few distractions from my children and nephews I was glad to be able to follow the entire megillah from Dad's scroll. I also felt guilt and sadness that I had never attended shul with my father on Purim since my kids were born and followed through the scroll with him. I knew how happy that would have made him. I suppose I had wanted my children to be amongst their friends for Purim and support my own shul. The more time that passes, the more regret I have at things I should have done or handled differently. I promised myself that I wouldn't have the same regrets with my mother. I wound the scroll back, ready to be read on the following morning at my shul and we went upstairs for the party.

As mentioned, one is supposed to abstain from any celebrations during the year of mourning. I was not going to tell the children that they couldn't attend the party upstairs. As it happens, they had a great time. There was a fancy dress competition and a rodeo, which looked like great fun and there were hotdogs and other tasty things to eat. I stayed close with my mum and sister and we left as soon as the children were ready.

The next morning I went to Redbridge shul and used Dad's scroll again. I once again wound it carefully back up, placed it back inside the tube and put it back in the office at my mother's house where it remains until I use it again every year. I don't know why, but certain items that Dad left to me I feel more comfortable leaving at Mum's house.

8

I was becoming increasingly worried about my exhaustion. My grief was also not getting any better – if anything I was feeling worse every day. I recalled four years earlier when my mother's first cousin Alan had passed away. Alan had never married or had any children and had always been very close with my parents, sisters and myself. He regarded Mum more as a sister than a cousin and always kept a fatherly eye on me and took great interest and pride in my children. When Alan passed away, I became quite ill with depression. It was the first time in my life I had ever been diagnosed with this. It is not a chronic condition like my mother has but can be triggered through stress. When Alan passed away, I couldn't sleep at night and was in a constant battle trying to hide the condition from others. I finally went to the doctor and asked for help. The doctor said my inability to sleep was caused by underlying depression and prescribed me antidepressants, but also took mercy on me and gave me a month's supply of sleeping pills. Southgate Shul held a memorial service for Alan where I was asked to speak on behalf of the family. It was a beautiful service and a fitting tribute to such a gentle person who was so loved by his family and friends. I got even more stressed at the thought of having to speak publicly at such an emotional time. Somehow I got through it and sat down again next to my father.

At the time, my parents were getting concerned about me and asked me what was wrong. I finally admitted that I wasn't well and the doctor had prescribed antidepressants. Dad asked me when this started and I began to cry and told him the night Alan passed away. I'll never forget Dad's response. He said 'G-d knows what you'll be like when my time comes!' I remember thinking at the time that I couldn't possibly feel any worse. I was so wrong and as usual, Dad was right. The older I get, the more I realise how correct Dad was in all the advice he gave me over the years.

I went back to the doctor and described how I was feeling and the constant exhaustion I was suffering with. She asked me if I had suicidal thoughts. I said no. I knew I would never act on them and was also aware that she would be most likely bound by duty of care to report this piece of information. She agreed that the medication wasn't working and prescribed different pills. She told me that I needed to gradually come off the pills over a few weeks, reducing the dosage until I could start on the new pills. I decided to use the time away in Israel to come off them. At least I would be with my family if I started to feel worse.

I don't remember much about the time we spent in Israel for Pesach. Abigail reminds me that I was not even in the right frame of mind to pack my children's suitcases and that she had had to accompany me to my ex-wife's house to go through what clothes we would need. I have no recollection of this.

On reflection, I feel terribly sorry for David, who had to cope with a grieving wife, brother-in-law and mother-in-law. My strongest memory is of David organising a minyan for me on the plane so that I could say kaddish and of rushing around Ovda airport on our return trip, once again sorting a minyan for me. The trip was hard for all of us. We did our best to act as normally as we possibly could for the children but it was tough. Upon arrival, Mum took out a picture of Dad and placed it on her bedside table. Dad had organised and planned this trip and his absence was strongly felt. Seeing his photo was terribly difficult and I had to take some time alone on the balcony.

I located the hotel shul, which was situated in the basement. As promised, Abigail and David looked after my children so that I could still get to recite kaddish at least once per day. The congregation was mainly French and the service was Sephardi – I was unfamiliar with the order of the service but again was just relieved that I could attend and that the people were welcoming.

I was missing Emma, Aviv, my niece Sophie and my nephew Sam. They were unable to be with us as they had booked many months earlier to go to Croatia for Pesach with the family to celebrate Aviv's mother's 70th birthday. I was worried how Emma would be coping and really missed her that year.

Seder night was emotionally difficult for all of us. Dad had always loved Pesach and enjoyed a large seder. I got out Dad's frog and placed it on the seder table. The evening progressed and most people seemed to do their own thing as did we. We started off in unison until the expected 'balagan' commenced. It was during dinner that a fist fight broke out on the table next to ours. Looking back now I find it quite amusing but at the time I was shocked. A large Israeli family had a disagreement. There must have been twenty of them around the table. An argument broke out between a husband and his wife, which led to the father telling off the son-in-law for speaking to his daughter in that way, which led to the son-in-law punching the father-in-law in the face, which led to another son going for the brother-in-law. At this point, chaos descended in the room as the fight got more serious and came towards our table. David rushed the children outside the dining room and I stood in front of my mother who was still seated at the table, ready to fend off anyone who got too close to her. The fight did indeed reach our table and the entire table with all its contents crashed to the floor. The fight was eventually stopped and I turned around to check Mum was ok and couldn't find her. She eventually turned up and when I asked her where she had been she said that she had felt it was a good opportunity to go over to the dessert buffet as everyone was occupied!

I was very snappy with the children during our time away. Constantly telling them off and very impatient. I felt and still feel very guilty because of this. I hope they will understand that it was not an easy time for me and hope-fully I've made it up to them on subsequent trips to Israel. However, it was the nicest experience to come down to breakfast every morning and see Mum there. My children and their cousins, Jonah and Gabriel, have always got on amazingly well and it was a huge help to me that they could keep each other occupied for such a long time and give me a break. I have always got a lot of strength from my family and to spend ten days together with them did me the world of good. I was also using this time to come off the medica-tion and that may have also affected how I was feeling.

Dad had loved the state of Israel. We had always holidayed there as children and I had lived there for four years in my early twenties. In later years he loved holidaying in Eilat with Mum. We have managed to go back to Israel for Pesach as a family every year since Dad passed away. The following year I decided that I would collect some stones from the Red Sea and since then, every time Mum and I visit Dad, we have placed these stones at his grave. I took way too many stones and had to explain myself at the secu-rity check on our way home.

As much as I was initially against the idea, I was really grateful to my mother for insisting that we went to Israel after all. I look forward all year round to this special time with my family.

9

Arriving back in England was tough. It was then that I real-ised how much I had needed a change of environment and how nice it had been to spend that time with my family.

I had come off the antidepressants and noticed that my exhaustion seemed to have vanished. I came to the conclusion that the pills had not been the right ones for me and decided not to start with the new ones. My grief was still just as strong and I did my best to keep myself busy. I had been invited to join the shul's board of management, which I had accepted. I was still attending every service and spending most of my days at Mum's place, sorting through Dad's estate. Mum continued to stay at my place on Monday and Tuesday nights. I can never fully express my gratitude to her in enabling me to still get to Shacharit on the mornings I had the children. She seemed to mentally be getting stronger whereas I was getting weaker. Every now and then, when I took Mum shopping we usually ended up in Torah Treasures, browsing through the books and I would usually end up purchasing something.

Two books that I found really useful at this time were *Kaddish – Its Origins, Meanings and Laws* by Harav David Assaf and *The Neshama Should Have an Aliyah* by Rabbi Tzvi Hebel. I was also spending time reading through my parents' extensive Jewish book collection.

I was feeling immense guilt that my father had not had the confession recited for him leading up to his death. I blamed myself for panicking when Mum had suggested it. I had recited it next to him in the hospital after he had passed away but I knew that I had denied him this very important prayer. I spoke with Rabbi Wilson about it. He reminded me of how many people die suddenly without having the confession recited and told me it certainly was not the most important thing and my reaction at the time was understandable. This did make me feel slightly better.

Rabbi Wilson was always asking me to eat with him and his family on Shabbat and the Chaggim. I gladly accepted and came to regard him as a close friend and support during my year of mourning. His parents often came down from Manchester for the Chaggim – I had gotten to know his father a few years earlier when I joined the shul on a three-day trip to Poland to visit Auschwitz. Rabbi Wilson had led the group on a very special, emotional trip where virtual strangers bonded in an incredibly short space of time. He is a highly intelligent man with a wealth of knowledge in Halachic customs and Jewish law and also has a sharp wit and a great sense of humour. I always enjoyed my time spent with him and his family and I was very sad when he left the community.

Chapter 4
Depression

1

It is important to me that I write a little more about the effects of depression. This terrible condition has been present in my family for as long as I can remember. It can be a life-long condition that can fluctuate and may always need to be controlled by medication. Fortunately this has not been a life-long condition for me as it has sadly been for my mother. It is far more acceptable these days to speak about depression compared with previous generations where it was something to be swept under the carpet, surrounded by the stigma of shame. Medical research and treatment has also significantly improved over the years compared to rather barbaric methods used in the past such as constant sedation and even electric shock treatment. Far more men than ever before are speaking out on the subject – sharing their condition on social media and asking for support from their friends and loved ones. I greatly admire this. For me personally, it is not something I can easily talk about or discuss.

There have been three occasions throughout my life that I knew I needed to get help. The first was at the end of 2012 when I lost my cousin Alan. The second was in 2014 when my family were in the process of making aliyah – emigrating to live in Israel. I had not wanted to go and knew it was the wrong decision. I was extremely unhappy in my marriage but had agreed to go in the hope that my marriage may improve. I knew it was not going to – you take your problems with you and I had to go to the doctor again. Our aliyah lasted only six months before I asked for a divorce and we eventually came back to live in the UK. I have many regrets about this time in my life – my main one being that I should have refused to go and perhaps accepted earlier that my marriage was over, but as my children were involved, I wanted to at least explore every avenue. I am a great believer in fate and if I had not asked for a divorce and moved back to the UK, my children and I would have missed the last year of my father's life. Of course the third time was the period leading up to and after my father's death.

I find it difficult to admit that I may need help on occasion but I have accepted that I may suffer with this during exceptionally difficult times and can recognise the symptoms and ask for the help when it is needed. As far as opening up to people – I can confide in my immediate family but tend to shut off from extended family and my friends – completely shutting off from any form of social media or interaction. I can't see this ever changing. It may stem from my childhood where we were often warned never to discuss my mother's condition that may have left an underlying feeling of shame or weakness. Who knows? But I would strongly encourage anyone who feels they are suffering to at least speak with their doctor and try and confide in their closest family. For those who are comfortable enough within themselves to openly discuss any form of mental illness – you have my respect and admiration.

2

My parents had bought me a new set of tefillin for my forti-
eth birthday. It was a gift that I treasured. Shortly after my
father's death I started using his tefillin and weekday tallit
along with the bag that he carried them in. In many ways, I
found it extremely comforting. I found some Divrei Torah
(thoughts and commentaries on either the weekly sidrah or
an upcoming festival) that Dad had prepared to read out
at the seudah shlishit (the third meal on Shabbat – usually available for those who are attending the Mincha and
Ma'ariv service) at his shul. I kept them in his bag and occasionally would read through them. I still use Dad's tallit
and tefillin to this day.

Upon arriving in shul for the morning service, it is cus-
tomary to recite some silent prayers before we begin the
Shacharit service. There is one paragraph in the siddur
(from the Talmud) that I always found comforting and
every morning would read the Hebrew and the English.
*Eilu Devarim – 'These are the things whose fruits we eat in
this world but whose full reward awaits us in the World to
Come: honouring parents, acts of kindness, arriving early at the
house of study morning and evening, hospitality to strangers,
visiting the sick, helping the needy bride, attending to the dead,
devotion in prayer, and bringing peace between people – but
the study of Torah is equal to all of them.'*

My father had been a kind and honest man, leading his life
as an orthodox Jew, never bragging about acts of kindness
and charity and teaching me how to be humble in life. He
always reminded me that there was always someone who
was worse off than me and to be grateful for what I had.
The older I get, the more appreciative I am of the way my

parents raised me. It is with thanks to my father that I am capable of leading a service in shul, that I am capable of teaching my eldest son his barmitzvah. He showed me by example the importance of conducting yourself in business and in life with honesty and integrity.

The paragraph above which I read through every morning, emphasised to me that Dad had earned his place, along with any rewards in the World to Come.

The more reading I was doing, the more I was starting to understand my father's (his Neshama's) journey into the next world. The first year is a time of reflection. A time to reflect on one's life and how one may have handled situations in a different way. It is not about being judged for one's sins or transgressions. Nobody lives a perfect life. We all make mistakes, we can on occasion hurt others intentionally or unintentionally. This period of time is for the soul to reflect on their life and prepare for their ascent into heaven. I cannot emphasise enough, the importance of the acts of kindness made by the loved ones left behind – especially the children to help the soul on their journey. If my attending shul and reciting kaddish was even in the slightest way, helping my father's soul, then it was not in my nature to even question what I was doing. I knew my sisters were also taking on extra acts of kindness during this time.

I believe that the soul is very much between both worlds during the first year of passing away. I mentioned earlier that the soul mirrors the journey of the mourner and vice-versa. As my father was on a journey of reflection during this time, so was I. I came to the conclusion that my father had left this world, knowing that he had provided for and unconditionally loved his family, and as his twelve months of reflection came to an end, he would be less interested in the world he left behind, secure in the knowledge that he would be there to welcome us when our time came to part this world. I tried to explain to my children during this time that Zeide was now happy and no longer sick or in pain but it was difficult for us, in this world who were missing him so much. I get a lot of comfort from knowing that I will see Dad again when my time comes.

3

It was almost five months since my father had passed away. I had been unable to concentrate on anything except to survive each day, spend time with my family and go to bed each night and breathe a sigh of relief that I had said kaddish.

I started thinking more about my father's time spent at the hospital. There were so many aspects of his treatment that I was unhappy with and decided to write a letter of complaint. Before lodging a complaint, I usually decide what I hope to achieve. Nothing would bring my father back. I certainly didn't want any money but was hoping the hospital would acknowledge and admit their faults and hopefully put certain safeguards in place to ensure this kind of treatment did not happen again.

Even two and a half years after the events it still causes me a huge amount of anger and pain.

He received rough treatment from several male nurses who didn't warn him before checking his blood sugar, blood pressure and gave him a fright and caused unnecessary pain each time they jabbed a needle into him without warning.

Mum had strongly complained about this at the time but she received no follow up.

I wanted to know why they had felt it necessary to transfer my father to another ward the night he passed away and if indeed the time he passed away had been accurately recorded.

I raised all the points I mentioned earlier – the nurses not bothering to check on my father when I phoned up, concerned that he hadn't messaged me. The nurses who were supposed to be helping him but obviously were not near him when he fell to the floor after his stent operation. The doctor who advised my father that he could eat bread after his operation and the doctor the next day who said he should have never been told this. The doctor working alone on the ward who had no knowledge of my father's condition and would not be able to read his notes until at least 4 pm.

This was all so painful to set out in writing but I needed answers. I received an acknowledgement letter a few weeks later addressed to a Nicholas Rose. I couldn't believe that the hospital would make this further mistake and wrote back to them requesting that they could at least get my name correct.

I was shocked several weeks later to receive another letter apologising for their previous mistake – this time addressed to Mark Rose. I had no faith by this point that the hospital were going to treat my complaint with any level of seriousness.

I sent several letters throughout June and July requesting an update to my complaint. I received a response in July saying that they had set the complaints team a deadline of 11th August to respond. In fact it was not until half way through September that I finally received an official response. It was dated 13th September 2016.

My heart sank as I read through it. Phrases such as 'no recollection' and 'no evidence of complaints lodged' were a familiar theme throughout. I was well aware of the times I had complained about my father's treatment and the times my mother had complained – particularly about his rough treatment by the male nurses.

The biggest lie, which really shocked me, was their response to my father falling over. Their description of events 'after carefully interviewing the two nurses' was that my father became unsteady and they assisted him in a controlled way to gently sit on the floor as he could no longer support himself. This was a blatant lie and happened in front of my entire family. The nurses were nowhere near my father when he fell.

I had waited for four months for this response. I suppose I should have prepared myself for this but I wasn't. I cried as I read though their version of events and felt increasing anger to the point of rage.

I wanted to respond, pull them up on their lies and even look into the possibility of taking legal action if they failed to acknowledge this. I showed the letter to my mother after first explaining the contents. She was as hurt and angry as I was. I decided to wait a few days to calm down before reaching any decisions. I had a conversation with my brother-in-law's father, Charles, who had experienced a similar situation. He advised me to let the matter rest. The most likely outcome would be that I would not achieve anything and waste years pursuing this.

I decided to take his advice. I knew I did not have the strength to fight this matter and that each time I had to face this situation – which most likely would be drawn out over the years, I would be an emotional wreck. Nothing would bring back my father and I decided for the sake of my own sanity to let the matter rest. I did not even respond to the letter.

4

There are certain points during a year of mourning that hit you so incredibly hard. Birthdays, Shabbat, Jewish holidays, phoning the house and knowing that Dad would never answer the phone again, driving through Southgate High Street and still looking out for Dad, when you have good news to share, not receiving a call from Dad every Friday to give me a blessing. The list is endless.

When I was approaching barmitzvah age, my parents had started to buy me my own set of Machzorim (festival prayer books) for each upcoming festival. I use these books to this day. Dad suffered with arthritis – his fingers were very swollen and he found it difficult to grip a pen. Therefore, it was always Mum who inscribed my Jewish books, usually my name, Hebrew name, followed by the English and Hebrew date.

We were approaching the festival of Shavuot – celebrating the receiving of the Torah. Traditionally we eat dairy foods to symbolise purity. It is also one of the festivals where we recite the yizkor prayer in memory of our departed loved ones. I had never stayed in the service for yizkor. Apparently there is nothing wrong in doing so but I hadn't wished to remain and had always waited outside as many others had also chosen to do.

It is advisable, during the year of mourning not to attend the yizkor service as feelings are so raw and emotions running high. I decided to remain in the service.

On Erev Shavuot, as I was preparing to leave for shul, I took my Machzor from the bookshelf, opened the cover and to my amazement it was my father's writing. He had written my name, the word Shavuot in Hebrew script and the year 1991 and the Hebrew year – 5751. I was shocked. I couldn't remember Dad having done this, although at the time I most likely hadn't given it much thought. But I couldn't help be amazed that exactly twenty five years after Dad wrote in this book, I would be using it for the first time to say yizkor for him.

I went to shul and led the Mincha service and then sat back down again as we commenced the evening service. It didn't last long and I was soon walking home.

The next morning I arrived at shul for the start of the service. I was feeling worried that I wouldn't be able to remain composed during yizkor. As is the custom, two Sifrei Torah were removed from the Ark for the leyening. It was at the end of the leyening that I was called up to do Hagbaha (the lifting of the Torah). I didn't think much of it but as I sat down on the bimah with my arm around the Torah after it had been dressed, it suddenly dawned on me that I would need to stand on the bimah holding the

Torah during yizkor. I started to panic and looked around trying to get someone's attention. I don't recall if I managed to speak to anyone but it was to no avail and about ten minutes later I was standing in front of everyone, holding the Torah which was getting heavier and heavier with tears coming down my face, in full view of the congregation, trying to get through the service. As soon as I was able to hand the Torah back to the Chazan I made my way outside for some fresh air. Sometimes, setting out to do something, no matter how good our intentions are, can occasionally backfire. In retrospect I should never have been called up but I know it was an oversight. I had planned to go to a corner of the shul and recite the yizkor prayer alone. It was a horrible experience.

5

My savings were rapidly diminishing and I needed to return to work. My background is in facilities management but I knew that working those long hours again, would not enable me to spend the time I wanted to with my children. I was also determined to say kaddish for the full eleven months. I needed to find something more flexible. After several ideas I decided that becoming a driving instructor might suit me. I did some research and decided to do my training with Red Driving School.

I needed to fill out the relevant paperwork and get the necessary qualifications. The first test I needed to pass was a theory test – more in depth and aimed as much at teaching techniques as knowing the highway code and hazard perception. I put the time in to study, spending quite a bit of time reading up on the subject and doing mock tests on line. I passed the first test and then had to train for Part 2 – an advanced driving test.

Red assigned me a trainer and I had to learn how to drive 'safely' again. I had driven automatic cars for the better part of twenty years and had to get used to a manual car again and train towards taking the driving test. I found it really difficult – like most people, I had picked up a lot of bad habits over the years. Did this make me a dangerous driver? No, but I would not pass an extended driving test by driving in my usual fashion.

The day of the test arrived and I got in my car with the examiner at Goodmayes Driving Test Centre. She told me she would be expecting a very high standard of driving – standard talk for anyone taking this test. It lasted an hour and incorporated an emergency stop, every manoeuvre that was currently on test, motorway driving and independent driving. I was very relieved when it was over and to be told I had passed.

The most intense part of the training was now about to start. I had to learn how to teach, how to deliver a lesson suitable for whatever stage a learner had reached – whether they were a complete novice or approaching test standard. There was a lot of role-play involved with my trainer playing the part of a student driver through different stages of their training. I had to complete a minimum of twenty hours of training, not including coursework that I had to complete in my own time.

I was feeling pleased that I was heading towards a new career that would suit my commitments to my children but emotionally I was still feeling the same.

6

My mother's birthday was approaching. I was getting concerned about how Mum was going to be able to cope on this day – waking up without Dad to wish her a happy birthday. Dad had usually taken Mum out for lunch to celebrate her birthday or we had all gone out together somewhere. I knew this was going to be an exceptionally difficult day for all of us. I couldn't take Mum out to celebrate. Firstly, I would miss the Mincha service and secondly, because I was not able to take part in celebrations. If I am being totally honest, I couldn't even contemplate celebrating anything at that stage. It was just too hard and Mum felt the same.

I should also mention that a twelve-month mourning period is only applied for a parent. Every soul should have kaddish recited for them for eleven months but as far as the mourning period goes, only a parent is supposed to be mourned for one year. The reasoning behind this is to acknowledge the sacrifices a parent makes in raising their children – the struggle, sacrifice and unconditional love, which goes far beyond childhood. Death can affect people in so many different ways. For me personally, I needed this year of mourning. If I hadn't had shul to attend, a reason to set my alarm and get out of bed every morning I don't know what I would have done. Throughout this year, as much as I was struggling, I had a purpose. I had a routine that the rest of my life had to work around. To take it one step further, I was fulfilling my obligation to my father. He had desperately wanted a son to say kaddish for him and it seemed to me that the biggest honour I was able to show him was in the year after he passed away.

Although the mourning period for a parent lasts for twelve months, kaddish is only recited for eleven months. The reason for this is that the departed should have done enough good deeds in their life to earn their place in the World to Come. To say kaddish for the full twelve months would be implying that they had not lived the best of lives.

On the morning of Mum's birthday, I went to Southgate Shul. It was Rosh Chodesh Tammuz (a new month in the Jewish calendar) so the service was starting earlier than usual. I was often the first person to arrive and I would go into the Beth Hamedresh, turn on the lights and usually read through one of Dad's Divrei Torah until it was time to put on his tefillin. Straight after shul I drove round the corner to Mum. I was feeling particularly emotional on this day. I opened the door and walked in. Mum was in the kitchen and I wished her a 'happy birthday' and broke down. She was great as always, we hugged and she told me it was a difficult day and she made me a coffee and we chatted for a while.

I had come to rely on Mum so much. She was the most stable person in my life at that point and even up to now. She cared so much about me and was willing to do whatever she could to support me in my grief and to help me continue to say kaddish.

On one occasion I mentioned to Mum that I kept running out of change (it is traditional to give to charity at every morning service – except on Shabbat of course). The next day, she went down to the bank and got me a bag full of change and told me that I could give to Tzedakah on her behalf as well. It is acts of kindness such as this that make her so special to me. Between my sisters and I, we were making sure Mum was ok and visiting as much as we could. But Mum was looking after all of us and was there for us as much as we needed her.

I can't remember what we did on the day. Most likely I took her shopping and we probably popped into Torah Treasures again to browse through the books. The most important thing was that we were together.

7

The summer holidays were approaching. I had no plans to take the children away and was about to move house. I had wanted for some time to move closer to the shul and to the community I was growing close to. I had found a suitable place, originally a bungalow that at some point had an upstairs built. It was very spacious but more importantly was in the location that I wanted in Clayhall.

The children were going away with their mum in the middle of August so I arranged the moving date around this time. My mother and Abigail were on hand on moving day to help and between us we got quite a lot of unpacking done. Obviously, moving home can be stressful and there were quite a few problems when I first moved in. The kitchen floor had developed a leak under the floor boards and was on the point of collapse and I had to spend quite a bit of time cleaning and dusting and doing my best to kosher the kitchen but I got there in the end. I was still attending shul around the move and spent most evenings at Mum's place for dinner and would arrive back home after Ma'ariv and continue to unpack.

My newly acquired book collection had become very important to me and I had plenty of space to have them on display and refer to them when I needed. I also had plenty of pictures and canvases made up of the family.

I settled in fairly quickly and looked forward to the boys arriving back. Mum was finding it increasingly difficult to manage the stairs. The only toilet upstairs was an en suite off my bedroom, which wasn't really practical. I purchased a double blow-up bed so that she could sleep downstairs but after the first night it was clear that she was having difficulty getting up from it. The last thing I wanted was for her to feel uncomfortable and I recall one night dismantling my son's bed, carrying it downstairs and reassembling it for her.

We visited some bed shops but did not find anything sturdy that could also be stored away. Finally, we found what we were looking for in a catalogue. A blow-up bed that was on legs that folded up and was stored in a bag. We purchased it and I gave it a try when it arrived and it was comfortable for her. I always liked it when Mum referred to my house as her second home – which indeed it was.

8

My sister Abigail's birthday also falls during the month of August. This year it fell on Tisha B'av. The festival falls on the ninth day of the Jewish month of Av. It is the saddest day of the year, commemorating the destruction of the first and second temples in Jerusalem. I'm sure Abigail had no real desire to celebrate her birthday but I'm sure David and the children did what they could to make her feel special.

I arrived at Shul and after the evening service we read the *Book of Eicha* (Lamentations). The following morning one does not put on tallit or tefillin. We commenced the morning service, which was followed by us sitting on the floor and reading Kinot (a long selection of elegies composed after the many tragedies that have befallen the Jewish people) which Rabbi Wilson led us through.

The tallit and tefillin are put on for the afternoon service. It was a long day but I was glad to be with the Redbridge community.

The boys arrived back and were pleased with what I'd done with the house. I did as much as I could to keep them entertained. We went on trips to Southend-on-Sea and played golf and went bowling amongst other things. The new school year started and allowed me to carry on with my instructor training.

I needed to book in my Part 3 test. This would involve the examiner playing the part of a student. I would be given two different scenarios, which would last thirty minutes each. The examiner would play the part of a novice student who I was meeting for the first time and I would need to follow on from any previous training given. The second part would be the examiner playing a different person who was reaching driving test standard but still needed to brush up on certain situations such as anticipation and hesitancy. I needed to work out what questions to ask, to plan the lesson and work out previous experience but also show that I could keep the lesson under control (the examiner would make constant, deliberate mistakes) and mark me on how I kept us safe and worked through any problems and issues until they were fully resolved. I would also be marked on the quality of briefings at the beginning of each lesson. Quite a lot for me to be getting on with.

At the beginning of September I also needed to have some minor surgery. I had had a small lump on my scalp for a while. I had asked my father to have a look whilst he was in hospital. He had said it was most likely a cyst but it seemed to be increasing in size and I decided to have it checked out. The doctor recommended that it was removed and analysed. An appointment was made for me at the Loxford Polyclinic in Ilford.

I was planning on going alone but Mum insisted on coming with me. On the morning of the surgery I went to Shacharit at Southgate shul and picked up Mum and we came back to my place and got a cab to the hospital. They called me in and the doctor went through the usual potential risks with me and I had to sign some papers.

I was given a local anesthetic and the doctor went to work. It was causing me an incredible amount of pain and I kept telling the doctor that she hadn't given me enough pain relief. I could feel every cut and tug and felt like I was going to pass out. Eventually she gave me more anesthetic and carried on. I told her I could still feel everything but she said it wouldn't last much longer. The process took about thirty minutes. I could feel the blood dripping down the back of my head and she then started to stitch my scalp back up. I was surprised at the huge amount of blood left on the bed and down my back. I did my best to clean myself up with some paper towels and went outside to my mother in the waiting room. I was in a lot of pain and feeling very nauseous and had to sit down for about twenty minutes and I asked Mum to give me some of her water.

Eventually I felt calmer and we went downstairs and ordered a minicab back to my place. Mum was planning on staying over. I went straight to bed for a few hours and when I woke up I was feeling a lot better and drove her home and then went back to shul and straight to bed.

The next morning my alarm went off at the usual time and I went to shul. I realised then that I couldn't put the head part of my tefillin on as it was placing the leather straps straight across the stitches. I left it off which is what I had to do for the next two weeks until the stitches came out. I was starting to feel really groggy and unsteady on my feet. I managed to stand up for kaddish but had to spend the service sitting down and was unable to look at my siddur. I spent the rest of the day at home resting and only went back out again for the evening service.

The analysis came back a few weeks later. It was nothing serious.

9

The Yamim Noraim (The High Holy Days) were coming up. I went with Mum to Marlow Road and to Waltham Abbey once again. Although I was dreading my father's upcoming stone-setting in November I would be glad when there would finally be a memorial in place rather than a mound of earth.

I had been reading though the Rosh Hashanah Machzor to give me more of an insight into the meaning of the two days spent in shul. I had already decided that I would not be celebrating a sweet new year. I couldn't – no matter how much of a mitzvah this is. I was going to be alone for Rosh Hashana. I had received an invitation to eat with Rabbi Wilson and his family, which I gladly accepted and we would go with the community to Tashlich later on that day. Tashlich comes from the Hebrew word which means 'to cast' – casting away our sins. Traditionally one throws pieces of bread into a river or stream whilst reciting special prayers. My understanding is that it is not the act of casting away our sins, but our solemn intent on reflecting on any transgressions we may have committed during the year and repairing our relationship with G-d that is most important. The period between Rosh Hashana (the Jewish New Year) and Yom Kippur (the day of atonement) is a very solemn time of reflection and asking for forgiveness.

As far as dipping the apple in honey, eating honeycake and traditional sweet items, I was not prepared to do this. At that stage I could not contemplate a happy new year, or any happy, sweet moment in my life without my dad.

Mum had decided to stay at home for Rosh Hashana and I was feeling sad and emotional. I hugged her goodbye and tried my best to wish her 'L'shana Tova'.

I arrived at shul on the Sunday evening. People were in a jovial mood and greeting each other enthusiastically. I made my way to the back of the shul. I was finding it hard to hold back my tears. Another member of the congregation arrived who unfortunately had recently lost his mother. We saw each other and hugged. I was hoping I would not be asked to lead the Mincha service as I didn't think I would have been able to. The Rabbi arrived, noticed the state I was in and I believe he may have requested that the warden should not to ask me to lead the service.

It was just a matter of getting through the next two days. The service is long on Rosh Hashana and I spent a lot of time walking back and forth from shul.

As always, it was nice to have lunch with Rabbi Wilson and his family before it was time to go to Tashlich. As far as meals went at home when I was by myself, I always tried to prepare something simple such as some salmon with potato salad that I could just help myself to.

I was glad when the days were over and I could call Mum to check she was ok.

Eight days later it was Yom Kippur – the holiest day of the year. We fast for twenty-five hours, and spend the entire day in shul, immersed in the spirituality of the day and hope that Gd will accept our repentance, forgive our sins, and seal our verdict for a year of life, health and happiness.

I had been asked to do the Haftorah on that day which I had accepted. I went to Shul for Kol Nidrei – again remembering the days that I had sat next to my father at this service. It lasted for around three hours and I walked home and went straight to bed.

I arrived at shul as usual first thing the next morning. It was of course going to be a long day and the shul was going to be packed later on. It was time for me to do the Haftorah and I got through it, singing as loudly as I could for the packed hall.

It was then time for yizkor – at least I knew I would not be required to be on the bimah this time. We started reading through the silent prayers, everyone thinking of their departed loved ones. Of course my focus was on my father.

'Yizkor Elokim Nishmas, Avi Mori, Mordechai Moshe Ben Arieh.' May G-d remember the soul of my father, my teacher, Mordechai Moshe Ben Arieh. I remembered saying the words 'Avi Mori' around the Shabbat table as a boy during the Benching (Grace after meals). I had said these words almost mechanically without much thought throughout the years. But finally, on this holiest of days, those two words, My father, my teacher, resonated in my heart and soul. It was at that moment that I realised my father had been the most important teacher of my life. The most important lesson Dad had taught me this year, was that it was never too late to try and better yourself. Again, I thanked G-d for giving me the best parents I could have ever wished for and for blessing me for forty-two years with Dad's presence.

I was glad when the service was finally over, finishing with the blast of the shofar. Everyone started to leave, but fortunately, enough people stayed back so that I could lead the Ma'ariv service and say kaddish once more. I drove home and called Mum to make sure she was ok and tucked into some bagels.

10

The next festival, Sukkot was upon us. Sukkot takes place five days after Yom Kippur and celebrates the gathering of the harvest and commemorates the protection G-d provided for the children of Israel when they left Egypt. Traditionally we build a sukkah (a makeshift hut) which one is supposed to eat and sleep in during this festival. The sukkah is made up of at least three walls and a roof (typically bamboo) and is set up under the open sky. Another observance is the taking of the 'four species' (Arbah Minim) – an etrog (citron), a lulav (from a palm tree), three hadassim (myrtle twigs) and two aravot (willow twigs). I bought mine from a stall in Golders Green Road and collected the willow from Uplands Road in Southgate by Pymmes Brook where I had accompanied my Father when I was a child to do the same thing. We had also performed the Tashlich service together at this location.

I was not able to have my own sukkah that year but was able to eat in one on most days with invites to Rabbi Wilson, having kiddush in the sukkah at Redbridge Shul and with invites to eat at both my sisters homes during the Chol Hamoed period. It was a special time once again seeing the children together.

It was during this time that I acquired another book. *My Father, My Mother and Me* by Yehudis Samet. A compilation of stories told by Sons and Daughters of their devotion, challenges and success in honouring parents. The halachos was told by Rabbi Yehudis Samet.

Kibbud Av Va'eim (honouring one's parents) is one of the Ten Commandments. I found this book fascinating. It dealt with how we can understand and observe this never ending mitzvah from childhood into adulthood.

The more I read, the more I understood that one can never show enough respect to a parent. Some of the stories of devotion sincerely humbled me. I reflected back to my teenage years. Had I always been a respectful son? Of course not. Had I always jumped at any request from my parents? No. Did they know that I loved and respected them? Yes. I sometimes feel guilt when I look back at certain situations that I know I could have handled better. As a teenager and in my early twenties, as I suspect with most young adults, I always felt I knew best. I had an arrogance that had not yet been tested with life's challenges. As I got older and became a parent myself, the more I understood the sacrifices my parents made to raise their three children in a loving, orthodox household. My father passed away knowing how much he was loved and just as importantly, we all knew how much he loved us.

The older I get, when I speak to my children, from telling them to turn the television softer to the words of advice that I give them, it's my father's voice that I hear coming from my mouth. Part of his soul has now joined my soul and will remain with me always.

If I have learnt anything from losing my father and through my year of mourning and continuous grief is that I cherish the time I get to spend with my dear mother. I can never show her enough respect. I can never do too much for her and always do my best to ensure that she knows how loved and respected she is. I pray that she will grace us with her presence, love and wisdom for many years to come.

11

The last of the festivals (Shemini Atzeret and Simchat Torah) were coming up. Shemini Atzeret is a stand-alone festival where we recite the prayer for rain and the yizkor service is once again recited. It is my Grandmother Lily's yahrzeit on Shemini Atzeret and I wished my mother a 'Long Life' prior to Yom Tov.

I was not looking forward to Simchat Torah – a time of celebration – reaching the end of the reading of the entire Torah throughout the year (V'zot Habracha) and starting over again (Bereshis). I was only attending shul on this day to recite kaddish but I had to hang around for the celebrations. As a mourner I was not allowed to participate, dancing around the shul, holding a Sefer Torah which I was thankful for. If I could have left early I would have but the service continued after the dancing.

I consumed too much whisky, which was not the brightest idea and I went back to the Rabbi's house for lunch before it was time to return to shul for Mincha and further celebrations. I managed to have a nap at the Rabbi's house and decided not to have any more alcohol.

We arrived back at shul and the dancing continued and foolishly, I drank more whisky, alone outside the main service. A member of the congregation came over to me and saw I was having a tough time keeping my composure. I explained how difficult I was finding any Jewish holiday or indeed any celebration. I spoke a little about my father and the tears flowed again. I am not sure if the whisky had made my mood better or worse.

I felt a sense of relief when the Yamim Noraim were finally over and I could continue with a sense of normality.

Chapter 5
Looking to the future

1

My instructor training continued. I was starting to understand how to deliver a lesson and how to prepare for the scenarios I was likely to be given on my test. After you have completed twenty hours of training you are allowed to start working on a training licence. The idea of the licence is not to work full time but to start getting used to real life situations and interactions with students and further prepare you for the final exam. Not everyone chooses to do this but I felt it was the correct step for me.

I needed to choose a suitable car for teaching in. Having driven large automatic cars for the better part of twenty years I now needed to choose something smaller. A lot of franchisees hire their cars as part of their franchise agreement. This costs a huge amount of money and anyone in this situation would need to work a lot of hours before even starting to make any profit. At the time, the car of choice for Red was the Vauxhall Corsa, this was followed by the Mini Cooper and is now the Renault Clio. Fortunately I was in the position to choose my own car and not hire one.

Red had strict guidelines on what cars could be used with their brand. Most cars that fell into the 'supermini' category were suitable. At the time, I felt Red believed that one could only teach in a small car. I later realised that it was all about their decals and what cars the decals would look good on.

After looking around I chose the Nissan Note. I liked the all-round cameras it had which would make it easier for me to teach the required manoeuvre's. I arranged collection and also to have the dual controls installed. My first day of teaching was going to be in December after I had completed a business seminar.

My nephew Sam's (Emma and Aviv's son's) barmitzvah was coming up. Emma had decided to postpone the party until after the year of mourning was up – an understandable decision. The barmitzvah was going to take place on the 10th of December and the party on the 2nd of January.

This was going to be the first major celebration in the immediate family since our father passed away. Dad's first born grandson's barmitzvah. His absence was going to be strongly felt.

Meanwhile, we first had to get through the stone-setting.

2

My father's headstone was ready and was going to be put in place a few days prior to the stone-setting ceremony. The stonemason had sent me a picture of it from the workshop but the quality of the picture was so awful that I couldn't tell what it was like.

I spent many weeks deciding what I would talk about on the day and kept making notes and gradually wrote about four pages, making constant revisions.

This was so important to me to get right. I had spoken briefly at the funeral with no time to prepare anything and certainly not being in the right frame of mind to speak. I had also spoken at the siyum at Southgate Shul marking the end of the shloshim.

This time I wanted to really speak in the most loving terms about Dad – what he had meant to me, the lessons I had learnt from him, his influence on me throughout my life and how his passing had changed my outlook on life and death and to mention how my sisters and I could still do good deeds in his memory and to his merit.

A few days beforehand, the stonemason emailed me a picture of the headstone in place. Mum was at my house at the time and the children were there. In my mind it was beautiful but the shock and sadness of seeing my father's name for the first time on the actual headstone was a moment, like so many other moments during the year that was too difficult to fully comprehend.

I gathered myself and then quietly asked my mother into the other room to view the headstone. It was a very emotional moment. The next day we went to Waltham Abbey to view it for ourselves for the first time. You can see it from quite far away, even from the car park if you know where to look. I knew that I needed to prepare myself for the flood of emotions before the actual stone-setting. I was holding Mum's arm as we walked towards it. To this day I still feel utter grief each time that I see Dad's name on the headstone but I know that it is a suitable monument to him and something I am proud of. I also see the blank space below my father's inscription, knowing that one day that blank space will have to be filled in – another reminder that nothing lasts forever and to cherish the time we have with our mother and bubba.

The day of the stone-setting arrived. I had given Natan the choice of whether he would like to come or not. I remembered I was thirteen when I attended my Grandma Malka's stone-setting at Marlow Road. I can still recall holding my father's hand when I saw the tears in his eyes. Dad and I have always been very similar in being unable to hold back on our emotions. Natan was ten at this point and I still felt he was too young. His zeide's death had affected him in a very bad way and I was worried about how he would cope and also how I would manage if he needed my attention. Natan decided not to attend, which I felt was the right decision.

I arrived about forty minutes before the stone-setting and met Emma, Aviv and my mother there. We went to the headstone and started cleaning it ensuring it was as presentable as could be.

Family and friends started to arrive and we made our way into the hall. There was a large turnout, which was pleasing to see. It was Remembrance Sunday and we held a minute's silence before the service commenced. We read through the prayers and then it was my time to speak. I composed myself and began reading. My nephew Sam stood at the podium with me for support. I got through it as best as I could and it was then time to recite kaddish. I closed my eyes as I always had and focused on my father and began.

My voice cracked a little half way through. We then filed out the hall and made our way to Dad's grave.

I walked with my mother, holding her arm and Rabbi Epstein walked the other side of me. He told me to look back at the crowd walking behind us and it was heartwarming to see so many people. We arrived at the stone and Rabbi Epstein read through the inscription, including a separate inscription from the grandchildren. It was then time for another kaddish. I was holding onto Mum as the ground was unsteady and I was worried that she may lose her balance. I held on to her arm and recited the mourners kaddish again, comforted to have her at my side.

The service was then over and people started to leave. We were all feeling drained and yet I was relieved that there was now a fitting memorial stone to my father rather than the pile of earth I had seen for the past ten months.

3

Sam's Barmitzvah date was on 2nd December. He would be leyening the sidrah, maftir and haftorah. His Hebrew birthday was on 26th November and he would be getting his first aliyah (call up to the Torah) then. I very much wanted to be there to witness this on behalf of my father and spoke to my sister and got myself invited for Shabbat along with our mum.

My sister made a very nice Friday night dinner after shul. We set off early to get back there on Shabbat morning. I was thinking of my father on the day as usual. The service started and I recited the kaddish prayer. It was a very emotional moment witnessing Sam's first call up. After the service we went back to Aviv's parents for lunch and stayed there until it was time for me to get back for Mincha – accompanied by a lot of the family.

I was glad we had stayed and was looking forward to hearing Sam leyening his sidrah in a few weeks' time.

4

I was coming to the end of my eleven months of saying kaddish. My final kaddish would be at the Mincha service on Tuesday 29th November. It dawned on me that this was the date I was supposed to be attending the business seminar. There was no way I could contemplate missing the last day of kaddish and had to postpone the two-day seminar until December which meant I had to put off my start date until the 9th of January 2017.

For eleven months my life had been consumed with attending shul, finding a minyan wherever I could and ensuring I could say kaddish. My life had completely changed and I was unsure of what life would hold for me after this.

My mother stayed over at my place on the Monday night as usual so that she could get the children ready for school and I could go to Shacharit. My shul did not hold a Mincha service but I had asked members of the congregation to attend as I wanted to be amongst people I was comfortable with.

My mother had said she would like to attend as well. She said it was important to her to witness me say my final kaddish for Dad. In truth I think she wanted to be there to support me.

I was feeling quite ill the following morning as I got up at 5.40 am. I was as quiet as possible so as not to disturb Mum and went to shul. When I got home, I discovered my mother in a terrible amount of pain. She had fallen over during the night. I was shocked when I found out and asked why she had not called out to me when she fell or called me when I had got up in the morning. She said that she had not wanted to stop me from going to shul. I was really upset by this response – as important as kaddish was, my mother's wellbeing had to come first and I told her so.

I could see that Mum was in terrible pain and told her to call her doctor in Enfield and make an emergency appointment whilst I took the children to school. She managed to get one and I helped her into the car and drove her to the doctor. The doctor examined her and said there was bruising and no major damage which I was thankful for.

We drove back to my place and stayed there until it was time to go to Mincha. I tried to persuade Mum to stay at home but she insisted on coming and I helped her to the car again and I drove us to my shul.

We must have looked a right state as I had to help her into the building and sit her on a chair just outside the room where we would be davening and told her she was not to stand up.

Rev Gary Newman was in attendance and said some kind words and I started to lead the service. 'Ashrei Yoshvei Baytecha' – I only managed to say the first three words and I couldn't speak anymore. I felt the biggest relief that I had achieved saying kaddish for eleven months. But what was I now going to do to help my father. How was I ever going to stop mourning him and carry on with my life? The tears poured down my face as I led the service. To this day I don't know how I got through it but somehow I managed and I recited my last kaddish for him as clearly as I could. The service was over. I couldn't look at anyone. The tears wouldn't stop. Some people hugged me – others shook my hand. I then saw my mother who was also in tears.

There was nothing either of us could say. I helped her to the car and we drove to my house. She commented on what a warm, friendly congregation I was part of. I had to agree with her. I was fortunate at how welcome I have always felt at Redbridge Shul, Cockfosters and North Southgate Shul and how welcoming the members of Barnet Shul were to me during my year of mourning.

5

My mother was in even worse pain the following day. We were both starting to worry that this was more than bruising. I asked her to make another appointment at her doctor and I took her back there. This time she was examined by a different doctor, who told her that she had cracked four ribs. There was no fix for this except with strong pain management. I was shocked that the doctor on the previous day had not been able to diagnose this. It took her over four months to recover. It was heartbreaking to see her in so much pain and I felt tremendous guilt that this had happened in my house.

Unfortunately this was the last time that Mum stayed over. There was a step leading up to the bathroom that had caused her to trip over during the night. She could have banged her head on the side of the bath. It doesn't bear thinking about.

I decided that Mum was better off in her own home and as much as the boys and I would miss her staying over – I felt it was the right decision.

My sisters as always were fantastic during this time. Visiting as often as possible and ensuring her fridge was stocked with their cooked meals, buying her beautiful flowers on a Friday before Shabbat. I have always been incredibly proud of them both and I know Dad was too.

It is impossible to fully express my appreciation to my mother for the nights she stayed over and helped get the boys ready for school. I was also relieved that I did not suffer any physical illnesses during my year of mourning. I suffer regularly with tonsillitis – it usually knocks me out for at least two weeks at a time when I get it but during the year of mourning this never happened. Perhaps someone was looking out for me.

It was a strange feeling not being bound by attending every service. I still regularly attended Shacharit and Ma'ariv. For so long my life had revolved around service times that it was difficult to mentally free myself up.

To this day I wake up regularly at 5.30 am. I feel guilt on not getting up as soon as I wake up. I remember telling Mum shortly after my year of mourning was over, that the following day I was not going to set my alarm and was going to stay in bed. The next morning I automatically woke up at 5.30 am and got up and went to shul.

I had booked to leyen my barmitzvah sidrah on Shabbt 14th January at my shul. I felt that if I could leyen the first part of a sidrah then I could do an entire sidrah again. It took me months to relearn and I practised at every opportunity. Again, my father had loved listening to me leyen and even though it had been over twenty-five years since I had done this, I wanted to still make my father proud.

6

Sam's barmitzvah was on 10th December at Edgware United. We had booked to stay at the Premier Inn at Edgware on the Friday night. I was really looking forward to the family being together again. We arrived at the hotel at roughly the same time and the cousins instantly started playing together – in and out of each other's rooms. Emma had very thoughtfully left some gift baskets in our rooms.

We drove to shul and enjoyed the Friday night service. I felt strange for a long time not saying kaddish. Out of respect for what it means to me, I always make sure I respond to the kaddish prayer and refuse to engage in any conversation when it is being recited.

We went back to Emma and Aviv's house for a lovely dinner and then walked back to the hotel.

We arrived at shul the next morning and the rest of the family started to turn up. I was relieved that Mum wouldn't have to climb any stairs and could sit behind the mechitzah in the main service (a physical barrier separating the men's section and women's section of an Orthodox synagogue).

The leyening commenced and Sam did the most wonderful job. His pronunciation was perfect. I was honoured to be given an aliyah and to stand next to Sam. I couldn't help but think about how proud my father would have been. I had visited Waltham Abbey on the previous day and chatted to Dad about the latest news and reminded him that it was Sam's barmitzvah the following day. I am positive that Dad was there with us, listening with pride.

The Rabbi gave a wonderful sermon and although he did not directly reference my father, reading between the lines, he mentioned how Sam's learning and what he had achieved on the day was directly benefiting his zeide.

Family and friends had lunch together in the shul hall after kiddush. Aviv made a lovely speech. When he mentioned my father's passing, I tried very hard to compose myself, but saw Natan glancing at me with a concerned look on his face and did my best to show him I was ok – not very convincingly unfortunately.

Despite the absence of Dad at such an important event, the Shabbat was a very special occasion full of love.

Finally the twelve months of mourning were over. Did I feel different at all? Not really. It takes time. As it was a leap year, it was going to be another month until my father's first yahrzeit.

I was still preparing and training for my new career and spending as much time with Mum as possible. It is always when I start to think that I am feeling better that I am gripped by uncontrollable grief at the strangest of times. It can still happen to this day. I think of him all the time. When my children do something that makes me proud I feel heartbroken that I can't tell him about it.

7

Sam's barmitzvah party was on the 2nd of January. Unfortunately on the day of the party, Natan injured himself in the park by running into a metal pole. By the time he arrived at my house, the lump on his head had alarmingly swelled and he was feeling nauseous. As much as I hated to, I had to let Emma know he wasn't going to come and his mother took him to the hospital. Fortunately it turned out not to be serious.

The party was lovely. We arrived early for group photos and then went outside the hall for the reception. A projector had been installed in the hall that would show family pictures throughout the evening. When we were invited to enter the hall for dinner there was a lovely picture of my father on the screen. This proved too much for me to emotionally handle and I quickly went to the corner of the room to try and pull myself together. David's mother, Janice, noticed the state I was in and came over to me. I don't remember what she said but she was incredibly kind.

The evening was lovely. Some wonderful speeches were made and I was asked to make the toast to the Queen. Once the dancing started I did my best to join in. My year of mourning was over and yet I felt guilty. I was pleased that I joined in with the Israeli dancing for a while. I stayed next to Mum for much of the evening. She was still in terrible pain and I was just relieved that she was able to be there.

8

It was my birthday on the 6th January. I've never really been one for celebrating my birthday. These days I try to forget it. It's too close to the day my father passed away and is a sad reminder of the day I had a breakdown, two days before he passed away. I can't bring myself to open any cards until the day of Dad's yahrzeit is over.

I commenced with the driving lessons on the 9th January 2017. I was a nervous wreck during my first week. Looking back I'm surprised that most of my students stuck with me. I realised how woefully unprepared I was to be giving driving lessons in real-life situations with unpredictable students. I persevered and have built myself a good reputation and stay in touch with most of my students who have passed their tests. I'm in full control of the lessons I give and although it is exhausting mentally, it is also a very rewarding job and I love working for myself and no longer have to put on a suit and go to work in the city with all the politics involved with my previous profession. I'll never be rich doing what I do, but as long as I can pay the bills and be with my children that is all that matters to me.

On Shabbat, the 14th of January 2017 I leyened my bar-mitzvah sidrah, Vayechei. It marked thirty years since my barmitzvah at the Glencairn Manor Hotel in Bournemouth in front of my family, with my dad standing next to me. Back then I had needed to stand on a box to see the top of the Torah. I went to see Dad again at the cemetery the day before and told him that I would be leyening my barmitz-vah sidrah for him and I hoped he could be there to listen and take pride in me.

I had been practising for months and was as ready as I would ever be. The Torah was taken from the ark and I stepped onto the bimah and took the yad (the pointer) in my hand. I felt no nerves again and leyened to the best of my ability. As my sidrah is the last one in the Book of Genesis, it is traditional for the congregation to stand and recite 'Chazak Chazak Venitchazek' – 'Let us be strong, let us be strong and let us strengthen others as well.' My understanding of this tradition is that the Jewish people are strong when we stand together and can overcome the most difficult of circumstances with the strength and guidance of the Torah.

This time, the meaning was different for me. I had overcome my nerves and achieved something I never thought I would ever be able to do again. My father's guidance and strength had led me to this point in my life. When I had reached the worst of times, the love of my family and my faith in G-d had guided me through the worst year of my life and inspired me to better myself. I had also come to the realisation that when nothing else can help, when you feel so completely isolated from everything, caught up in your own grief and suffering – G-d will always be there to turn to. Sometimes, faith and the power of prayer is the only thing to keep you going.

I hoped Dad had heard me leyen. I know he would have been so proud of me as my mother was.

9

My father's first yahrzeit was on the 25th January. I had read the haftorah in shul on the Shabbat prior to the yahrzeit and had asked my mum, sisters and brothers-in-law if they could join me at Shacharit that morning and suggested we attended the service at Southgate Shul. I wanted my family with me for comfort and also to ensure that we had a good minyan. They were only too happy to and I contacted the shul and asked if they could put up a mechitza in the Beth Hamedresh. It is also traditional to make a L'chaim (a toast) on a yahrzeit and we organised some drinks and biscuits. I was glad we were meeting at Southgate. It was the community I had grown up in, Dad had loved the shul and the community had been very kind to me throughout my year of mourning.

I lit the yahrzeit candle the evening before and drove to Mum. I didn't want to be alone. I had dinner with her and we spoke about Dad and I eventually went to Ma'ariv at Southgate Shul before driving back home.

The next morning I left in plenty of time but there was a hold up on the North Circular. I was stuck in traffic for about ten minutes and started worrying that I would be late. Fortunately the traffic picked up and I arrived on time and saw Mum setting out the cups and drinks on the table outside the Beth Hamedresh.

I went inside and started putting on Dad's tefillin. It was comforting having my family there on such a difficult day. I led the service and once again said kaddish.

At the end of the service, Rabbi Epstein said some very kind words about Dad and gave a D'var Torah which as usual was followed by Kaddish D'Rabanan. We all went back to Mum's place and had some breakfast and chatted before getting in my car and driving to Waltham Abbey. We walked together to our father's grave and stood there in silence, all lost in our own thoughts. When I felt strong enough I recited the memorial prayer. To this day it pains me so much saying my father's Hebrew name during the memorial prayer. I don't think I will ever get used to it. We then quietly recited some psalms and I started cleaning the headstone.

We drove back to Mum and had lunch. I needed to start work after the Mincha service at Barnet Shul and gave Mum a hug before I left.

Epilogue

It is Sunday evening on the 26th of August 2018. As I reflect back on my year of mourning I realise today how far I have come and the journey I was on during that terrible year of 2016. To this day, I still can't put the James Bond ringtone back on my phone. My father left me his Rolex watch, which my grandfather Louis had purchased in the 1940's. I had it serviced and it remains in its box. I don't feel quite ready to wear it. Perhaps I will at Natan's barmitzvah. I still find it difficult to recite the Shema without that haunting image of standing over my father's body, stroking his hair whilst reciting the same prayer.

I'm thankful that none of us knew that Dad had pancreatic cancer until the symptoms worsened. There is nothing that would have effectively helped him at his age. Operating would have definitely been out of the question. I dread to think how any of us (Dad in particular) would have managed with this news. He certainly would not have gone to Israel. It astounds me that I was swimming in the Mediterranean Sea, in Israel, with my parents four months before Dad passed away, and I'll always be grateful for this time we had together.

The final text message I have on my phone from Dad was on the 20th December 2015 at 6.24 pm. I said 'Love you Dad.' He responded with 'Thanks I love you too xxx.' I'm glad this was our final message. I transferred all of his voicemails to my computer and sometimes play the odd message, wishing I could speak to him properly again. I do have lots of camcorder footage of him taken over the years but still find it too hard to watch for now.

I'm teaching Natan his barmitzvah sidrah. He's doing incredibly well and will be reading the sidrah, maftir and haftorah on 23rd March 2019 – Parashat Tzav. I know if my father were here, he would have the Tikkun out and be practising non-stop with Natan – telling all of his friends at shul how proud he is of him.

When we practise at Mum's house, Natan likes to wear Dad's baseball cap and sits in the office with me next to Dad's picture. He constantly asks me if Zeide would be proud of him. My usual response is 'You have no idea how proud he would be Natan.'

I'm dreading the day arriving and not having Dad standing on the bimah next to Natan. But I know he will be with us and I thank G-d that Mum will be there. As I practise most evenings with Natan, my thoughts go back to when I was twelve, sitting at the dining table with Dad, night after night practicing my barmitzvah sidrah with him. We had the odd disagreement if he corrected a mistake, which I was convinced I had not made. He sometimes got the tape recorder out and started winding it back and playing it if I disagreed with him. He was always right and grinned at my sheepish look. I wish so much that he could see the same disagreements with Natan and myself – this time recorded on an iPad rather than a tape recorder. I know that on the day, to be standing beside Natan as his father and his teacher will be a very special moment and something I hope he looks back on with the fondest of memories in the years to come.

I will be leyening my barmitzvah sidrah again this year in shul. I'll need to put in the time to practise once again but I wanted Natan to witness me leyen on the lead up to his barmitzvah.

I am teaching my son Yaniv, Anim Zemirot which he will hopefully perform on the day as well. Yaniv doesn't attend a Jewish school and he has practically had to learn to read Hebrew again with me from scratch. He is over halfway through and I'm sure he will be ready on time and I am hoping that he will start singing it in shul on the lead up to the day. When Natan and I go into the office to practise his leyening, Yaniv likes to practise Anim Zemirot in the lounge with Mum. We were driving home from her on Thursday and he told me that Bubba cried. I asked why and he said 'Because she was so proud of how I sung Anim Zemirot.' I am incredibly proud of both my boys and so fortunate to have a mum who takes so much interest and pride in her grandchildren.

My mother had another fall a few months back outside the doctors. It was a terrible shock and she had to go to hospital in an ambulance. Luckily she just suffered bruising this time. I have had a panic alarm installed at her home that she wears around her neck so in the event that she falls over she can press the alarm which will notify us and arrange an ambulance if necessary. I speak with her on the phone every day. I hate the fact that I can't get there as much as I used to – it's too difficult with work and the children but I make sure I take the kids to see her every week. I don't know how I would ever manage without her.

My father's yahrzeit next year will be on what would have been my parents 49th wedding anniversary.

I have much to be thankful for. I have two wonderful children, a very close family who are always there for each other. Natan's barmitzvah will be followed six weeks later with Jonah's barmitzvah and I am very much hoping that we will all be together again in Israel for Pesach next year (in between the barmitzvahs).

I am busy with work and get very little time to myself. My shul attendance has not been very good as of late. When I don't have the children I start work early and finish late.

The panic attacks are long gone. It is true that time is the best healer. I feel happiness again and take pride in my family and friends and am back on social media, which I also use to promote my business. The grief will never be gone but it is bearable and I can continue with my life knowing that I did the best that I could to honour my father.

I am well aware that the grief and desperation that I felt is not unique. But the journey I went on most certainly was. People lose and mourn loved ones every day. At the time, no words can help. The feelings of grief can be so overwhelming that I felt at the time that nobody could possibly understand what I was going through. As my friends have lost parents and loved ones over the past few years, I realised how woefully inadequate any words of comfort that I offered were.

At the time, I read through some forums on the effects of pancreatic cancer. I was particularly interested in those who were unable to cope with losing a parent so suddenly to this terrible disease. Many of the stories were similar. I got no comfort from the knowledge that I was not alone in my grief, but was able to empathise with many people who were describing their experiences. I was never strong enough at the time to be able to add my own comments to these forums.

There are plenty of books available on the customs associated with the mourning process and death from a Halachic perspective. I wanted to write this book, documenting my own feelings and experiences throughout that year, in the hope that it may provide a small amount of comfort to anybody who has suffered a bereavement. It is my sincere hope that I have been able to achieve this objective.

Thursday 11ᵗʰ October 2018. I recently had lunch on the first day of Sukkot with the new Rabbi of Redbridge Shul, Steven Dansky and his lovely family. I mentioned to him how I would love one day to start learning to leyen Megillat Esther and to read it from my father's megillah scroll. Tonight we start the first of our weekly sessions where he will be teaching me. I can still make Mum and Dad proud!

לזכרון

ר' מרדכי משה בן ר' אריה

נפטר כ"ז טבת תשע"ו לפ"ק

In memory of my beloved father,
Mark Maurice Rose, Mordechai Moshe Ben Arieh.

ת’ נ’ צ’ ב’ ה‘

I would like to thank the following people:

My publisher Gareth Howard, at Authoright, for his encouragement and support.

Simon Goulden for his invaluable advice.

Rabbi Ephraim Guttentag for checking the halachic accuracy of my work and for his kind words of assurance.

My sister, Abigail, for her constructive comments and suggestions – in her own words, 'The first time I read it was as Dad's daughter. The second time was still as Dad's daughter but through his eyes.'

My mother, Ruth, for her blessing and approval for me to release this book, and for the love she gives to all her family